THE RICHEST PERSON IN BABYLON

Evoking Quality Publishing

FOREWORD

This adaptation of a classic novel has been altered to fit the modern age. A bit of the language has been smoothed out, but the most important alteration is that this book is rewritten using the gender-neutral pronoun Ze/Zir so that all may place themselves back in time in the great age of Babylon.

This book changed my world for the better, and I hope it changes yours as well. I believe that we will have a healthier society if all are taught the ways of making coin.

— *The Author*

CONTENTS

BANSIR & KOBBI

Parable 1

BANSIR, the chariot builder of the Great City of Babylon, was thoroughly discouraged.

From the seat upon the low wall surrounding the property, ze gazed sadly at the simple home and open workshop where a partially completed chariot stood. Bansir's spouse constantly appeared at the open door. The furtive glances in the chariot's direction were frequent reminders that the meal bag was almost empty—a sign that it was already time to go back to labor and finish the chariot. Hammering and hewing, polishing and painting, stretching taut the leather over the wheel rims, and preparing the chariot for delivery so coins could be collected from the wealthy customer.

Nevertheless, Bansir's fat, muscular body leaned calmly on the wall. It may appear to an outside observer that Bansir had stopped working, but zir mind was in fact occupied working through a problem, with no answers making themselves known as of yet.

The scorching heat from the tropical sun, so typical of this valley of the Euphrates, beat down mercilessly upon everything below. Beads of sweat formed upon Bansir's brow and trickled down unnoticed to get lost in the jungle of chest hair. Beyond zir home towered the high terraced wall surrounding the palace of the Great Ruler of the City. Nearby, cleaving the blue havens, was the vividly painted tower of the Temple of Bel.

In the shadow of such magnificence was Bansir's simple home and many others, far less neat and cared for. Babylon was like this, a mixture of grandeur and squalor, of dazzling wealth and direst poverty, crowded together without plan or system within the city's protective walls.

Behind Bansir was the street—filled with the noisy and chaotic chariots of the wealthy shoving aside the sandaled tradespeople and barefooted beggars. Even the well-off ones were forced to turn into the gutters to escape the long lines of bonded servants, laden with heavy goatskin jars, carrying waters on "The Ruler's Business" that was to be poured upon the hanging gardens.

Bansir was too engrossed in zir own problems to hear or heed the confused and ever-present ruckus of the prosperous city. However, the unexpected twanging of strings from a familiar lyre aroused Bansir from deep reverie. Ze turned and saw the familiar, smiling face of Kobbi the Musician, Bansir's best friend.

"May the gods bless thee with great liberality, my good friend," began Kobbi with an elaborate salute. "Yet, it does appear that they have already been so generous that thou need not to labor. I rejoice in thy good fortune! More, I would even share with thee from thy purse which must be bulging, or else thou would be busy in thy shop.

"Now, hear me, my friend... take out but two humble shekels and lend them to me until after the noble person's feast tonight. Thou wilt not miss them until they are returned. For it will be such a short time."

"If I did have two shekels," Bansir responded gloomily while glancing down at the dusty ground, "to no one could I lend them, not even to you, my best of friends; for they would be my fortune, my entire fortune. No person lends out their entire fortune, not even to their best friend."

"What?" exclaimed Kobbi with genuine surprise. "Thou do not have one shekel in thy purse, yet sit like a statue upon a wall?

Why not complete that chariot, then? How else can thou provide for thy noble appetite? 'Tis not like thee, my friend. Where is the endless energy? Does something distress thee? Have the gods brought these troubles?"

"A torment from the gods it must be," Bansir agreed. "It began with a dream, a senseless dream, in which I thought I was a person of means. From my belt hung an elegant purse, heavy with coins. There were shekels which I cast with careless freedom to the beggars; there were pieces of silver from which I bought finery for my spouse and whatever I did desire for myself; there were pieces of gold which made me feel assured of the future and unafraid to spend the silver. A glorious feeling of contentment was within me! You would not have known me for being your hardworking friend. Nor would you have known my spouse, with a face free of wrinkles that gleamed with happiness. Ze was again the smiling youth of our early married days."

"A pleasant dream, indeed," commented Kobbi, "but why should such pleasant feelings from a dream turn my good friend into a glum statue upon the wall?"

"Oh, why indeed, my friend! Because when I awoke and remembered how empty my purse was, a feeling of rebellion swept over me. Let us talk it over together, for, as the sailors do say, we ride in the same boat, we two. As youngsters, we went together to the Holy Person to learn wisdom. As young people, we shared each other's pleasures. As grown individuals, we have always been close friends. We were content beings. We were satisfied to work long hours and spend our earnings freely. We earned much coin in the years that have passed. Yet to know the joys that come from wealth, we can only dream about them."

Bansir grunted and slapped zir knee, causing Kobbi to step back in surprise.

"Bah! Are we anything more than dumb sheep?" Bansir said, sighing. "We live in the richest city in the world. Travelers say none equals it in wealth. All around us is much display of wealth, and yet of it we ourselves have naught. Then you, my best of friends, after half a lifetime of hard labor and still an empty purse, approach and say to me, 'May I borrow such a trifle as two shekels until after the noble person's feast tonight?' What do I reply? Should I say, 'Here is my purse; its contents will I gladly share?' No, I admit that my purse is as empty as yours. What is the matter with us? What cannot we acquire, silver and gold—more than enough for food and robes?

"Consider, also, our children," Bansir continued, "are they not following in their parents' footsteps? Do they and their families and their children and their children's children live all their lives in the midst of such treasures of gold and yet, like us, be content to feast upon sour goat's milk and porridge?"

Kobbi had a puzzled look on zir face and said, "Never, in all the years of our friendship, did thou talk like this before, Bansir."

"Never in all those years did I think like this, either. From early dawn until darkness stopped me, I have labored to build the finest chariots. All while hoping someday the gods will recognize my deeds and bestow upon me great prosperity. This—they have never done. At last, I realized that they will never grant such a wish. Therefore, my heart is sad.

"I wish to be a person of means," Bansir continued. "I wish to own lands and cattle, to have fine robes and coins in my purse. I am willing to work for these things with all the strength in my back, with all the skill in my hands, with all the cunning ideas in my mind. Oh, how eagerly I dreamed that my labors would be fairly rewarded. What is the matter with us? Again, I ask you! Why cannot we have our just and right share of the good things so plentiful for those who have the gold with which to buy them?"

"Would I know the answer?" Kobbi replied. "No better than thou am I satisfied. My earnings from my lyre are quickly gone. Often I must plan and scheme so that my family is not hungry. Also, within my chest is a deep longing for a lyre large enough to truly sing the strains of music that surge through my mind. With such an instrument, I am bound to make music finer than any song the Great Ruler has heard before."

With a reaffirming tone, Bansir responded, "Such a lyre you should have. No person in all of Babylon could make it sing more sweetly other than you and not only the Great Ruler of the City, but the Gods themselves would be delighted. But how can you secure it while both of us are as poor as the Great Ruler's bonded servants? Listen to the bell! Here they come." Ze pointed to the long column of half-naked, sweating water bearers plodding laboriously up the city's narrow streets from the river. Five abreast they marched, each bent under a heavy goatskin of water.

"A fine figure of a person who does lead them," Kobbi said, pointing at the wearer of the bell who marched in front without a load. "A prominent person in their own country, 'tis easy to see."

"There are many good figures in the line," Bansir agreed, "as good people as we are. Tall, blonde person from the north, laughing black person from the south, little brown person from the nearer countries. All marching together from the river to the gardens and back, day after day, year after year. Naught of happiness to look forward to. Beds of straw in which they sleep. Hard grain porridge to eat. Pity the poor brutes, Kobbi!"

"Pity them I do. Yet, thou do make me see how little better off we are, free persons though we call ourselves."

"That is the truth, Kobbi, unpleasant thought it may be. We do not wish to go on year after year living slavish lives. Working, working, working! Getting nowhere. A lifetime of wasted effort."

"Do thou think that we can discover how others acquire gold and do as they do?" Kobbi asked.

"Perhaps there is some secret we might learn if we seek it from those who know," replied Bansir thoughtfully.

"This very day," said Kobbi, "I did pass our old friend, Arkad, riding in zir golden chariot. This I will say, ze did not look over my humble head as many in that station might consider their right. Instead, ze did wave a hand so that all the onlookers might see Arkad pay greetings and bestow a smile of friendship upon Kobbi the Musician."

"Arkad is claimed to be the richest person in all of Babylon," Bansir mused.

"So rich, the Great Ruler is said to seek Arkad's golden aid in affairs of the treasury," Kobbi added. "So rich..."

"I fear that if I meet Arkad in the darkness of the night," Bansir interrupted, "I might lay my hands upon zir fat wallet."

"Nonsense," reproved Kobbi. "A person's wealth is not in the purse carried upon the hip. *A fat purse quickly empties if there is no golden stream to refill it.* Arkad has an income that constantly keeps zir purse full, no matter how liberal the spending habits."

"Income, that is the thing," said Bansir. "I wish for an income that will keep flowing into my purse whether I sit upon the wall or travel to far lands. Arkad must know how a person can make an income for themself. Do you suppose it is something that could be made clear to a mind as slow as mine?"

"It seems to me that Arkad has already passed this wisdom upon zir eldest child, Nomasir," Kobbi responded.

"Did this Nomasir not journey to Nineveh and as was said at the inn, become—without any aid from zir parents—one of the wealthiest people in that city?"

"Kobbi, my friend, you have brought upon me a rare thought." A new light gleamed in Bansir's eyes. "It costs nothing to ask wise advice from a good friend and Arkad was always that. Never mind though our purses are as empty as the falcon's nest a year ago. Let that not detain us. We are weary of being without gold in the midst of plenty. We wish to become people of means. Come, let us go to Arkad and ask how we, also, may acquire income for ourselves."

"Thou speak with true inspiration, Bansir—you guided my mind to a new understanding. *It is now clear to me as to why we have never found a great measure of wealth is because we never sought for it.* Thou have labored patiently to build the most excellent chariots in Babylon. To that purpose were your best endeavors devoted. Therefore, at it thou did succeed. I strove to become a skillful lyre player. And, at it, I did flourish, my friend."

"In those things, toward which we exerted our best endeavors, we succeeded," spoke Kobbi. "The gods were content to let us continue thus. Now, at last, we see the light, bright as the rising sun. It inspires us to learn more so that we may prosper more. With a new understanding we shall find honorable ways to accomplish our desires."

"Let us go to Arkad this very day then," Bansir urged. "Also, let us ask our other friends from the young days who have fared no better than ourselves, they too shall join us so that they may share in the wisdom."

"*Thou are ever so thoughtful of thy friends, Bansir, and therefore, acquainted with many companions.* It shall be as thou say. We accomplish this desire to learn this very day in the present and take our friends with us."

ARKAD

Parable 2

IN OLD BABYLON, there once lived an extremely wealthy person beyond doubt, known as Arkad. Many said ze was the richest person in the city, and few could dispute this.

Arkad, the Richest Person in Babylon

Far and wide, this was a known fact to the people of Babylon —even the ones outside it. Arkad was famed as a person of exceptional wealth and great liberality, generous with charities and existing family. Ze was also independent in zir own expenses. Nevertheless, each year zir wealth increased more rapidly than it was spent.

And there were certain friends of younger days who came to zir and said, "You, Arkad, are more fortunate than we. You have become the richest person in all Babylon while we struggle for existence. You can wear the finest garments and enjoy the rarest foods, while we must be content if we can clothe our families in presentable raiment and feed them as best we can.

"Yet, once, we were equal. We studied under the same master and played the same games. And in neither the studies nor games did you outshine us. In the years since, you have been no more of an honorable citizen than we.

"Nor have you worked harder or more faithfully than anyone else, as far as we can judge. Why, then, should *Fickle Fate* single you out to enjoy all the good things in life and ignore us who are equally deserving?"

Thereupon Arkad remonstrated with them, saying, "If you have not acquired more than a bare existence in the years since we were youths, it is because you either have failed to learn the laws that govern the building of wealth or do not observe them. *Fickle Fate* is a vicious god who brings no permanent good to anyone. On the contrary, this god brings ruin to almost every person who they shower unearned gold upon. The god makes wanton spenders, who soon dissipate everything they receive and are left beset by overwhelming appetites and desires that they do not have the ability to gratify." Arkad paused and looked at them seriously as ze continued to speak. "Yet others whom *Fickle Fate* favors become misers and hoard their wealth, fearing to spend what they have, knowing they do not doom themselves to lives of emptiness and secret misery.

"Others, there probably are, who take unearned gold, add to it, and continue to be happy and content citizens. But so few are they, I know of them but by hearsay. Think now of a person who has inherited sudden wealth and see if these things are not so."

Kobbi's friends admitted that of the people they knew who had inherited wealth, many of them considered these words true and besought Arkad to explain how ze had possessed so much prosperity. So, Arkad continued, "In my youth, I looked about me and saw all the good things there were to bring happiness and contentment. I realized then that wealth increased the potency of all these. Wealth is power. With wealth, many things are possible.

"One may ornament their home with the richest of furnishings. One may sail the distant seas. One may feast on delicacies of faraway lands. One may buy the ornaments of the gold worker and the stone polisher. One may even build mighty temples to the gods. One may do all these things and many more in which there is delight for the senses and gratification of the soul."

With a subtle smile and a slight raise of head, Arkad said, "And, when I realized all these, I decided that I will claim my share of the finest offerings in life. I refuse to be one of those who stand far off, enviously watching others enjoy. I would not be content to clothe myself in the cheapest raiment that looked respectable. Nor would I accept the lot of the poor with quiet resignation. On the contrary, I vow to make myself a humble guest at this banquet of good things.

"Being, as you know, the child of a humble merchant—one among many in a large family with no hope of an inheritance—and not being endowed, as you have frankly said, with superior powers or wisdom, I decided that if I were to achieve what I desired, it would require both study and time.

"As for time, all people have it in abundance. All of us are born with it equally. And yet you, each of you, have let enough time slip by to have made yourselves wealthy. You admit that you have nothing to show except your good families, of which you may be justly proud.

"As for study, did not our wise teacher teach us that learning is of two kinds? One kind consists of the things we learned and knew, and the other is the training that taught us how to seek out what we do not yet know?

"Therefore, I decided to find out how one might accumulate wealth,

and when I have found it, I will make this my task and do it well. For, I believe, we should enjoy life while we dwell in the brightness of the sunshine. For sorrows enough shall descend upon us when we depart this world after death and enter the Land of the Darkness where we dwell among the spirits.

"I found employment as a humble scribe in the hall of records, and long hours each day I labored upon the clay tablets. Week after week, and month after month, I labored. Yet, for my earnings, I had nothing to show. Food, clothing, and penance to the gods, and other things—of which I could no longer even remember—absorbed all my earnings. But my determination did not leave me.

"And one day, Algamish, the money lender, came to the house of the city master and ordered a copy of the Ninth Law and ze said to me, 'I must have this in two days, and if the task is done by that time, two coppers will I give to you.' "

Algamish, the Money Lender

"So, I labored hard, but the law was long, and when Algamish returned the task was not yet done. Ze was angry, and had I been a bonded servant belonging to Algamish. A beating would surely have been dispensed. But knowing the city master would not permit zir to injure me, I was unafraid, so I said,

" 'Algamish, you are a very rich person. Tell me how I can also become rich, and all night I will carve upon the clay, and when the sun rises, the task shall be completed.'

"Smiling at me, Algamish replied, 'You are a forward rascal, but we will call it a bargain.'

"Thus, all that night I carved," Arkad continued, "though my back ached and the smell of the wick made my head ache until my eyes could hardly see. But when ze returned at sunrise, the tablets were completed. As Algamish arrived and I presented the tablets, I said, 'Now tell me what you promised.'

"Algamish laughed aloud and told me, 'You have fulfilled your part of our bargain, my child, and I am ready to fulfill mine. I will tell you the things you wish to know because I am becoming an old person. And an old tongue loves to wag. When youth seeks the advice of the aged, they receive the wisdom of years.

" 'But too often does youth think that aged knows only the wisdom of the days long gone, and therefore profit not. *But remember this: the sun that shines today is the sun that shone when your parents were born, and will still be shining when your last grandchild passes into the Land of the Darkness.*'

"As Algamish stared off remembering past days, ze continued, 'The thoughts of the youth are like bright lights shining forth like the meteors that often make the sky brilliant. But the wisdom of age is like the fixed stars that shine so unchanged that the sailor may depend upon them to steer a course. Mark well my words, for if you do not, you will fail to grasp the truth that I will tell you, and you will think that your night's work has been in vain.'

"Then ze looked at me shrewdly from under wrinkly brows and said in a low, forceful tone,

" '*I found the road to wealth when I decided that part of all I earn was mine to keep.* And so will you.' Then ze continued to look at me with a gaze that pierced me, yet said nothing more.

" 'Is that all?' I asked. Ze then told me,

" 'That was sufficient to change the heart of a shepherd into the heart of a money lender.'

"Still, I demanded, 'But all I earn is mine to keep, is it not?'

" 'Far from it,' ze said. 'Do you not pay the garment maker? Do you not pay the sandal maker? Do you not pay for the things you eat? *Can you live in Babylon without spending? What have you to show for your earnings of the past month? What for the past year? Fool! You pay everyone but yourself. You dullard, you labor for others. You might as well be a bonded servant and work for what your master gives you to eat and wear.* If you did keep for yourself, one-tenth of all you earned, how much would you have in ten years?' ze asked.

"My knowledge of the numbers did not forsake me, and I answered, 'As much as I earn in one year.'

"Then, Algamish replied, 'You speak but half the truth. Every gold piece you save is a bonded servant to work for you. Every copper it earns is its child that also can earn for you. If you are to become wealthy, then what you save must also earn, and its children must too. All of these together may help give you the abundance you crave.

" 'What? Do you think I cheat you for your long night's work?' ze continued. 'But I am paying you a thousand times over if you have the intelligence to grasp the truth I offer you.

" 'Remember, a part of all you earn is yours to keep. It should not be less than a tenth no matter how little you earn. It can be as much as you can afford, just never less. Pay yourself first. Do not buy from the clothes maker and the sandal maker more than you can pay out of the rest and still have enough for food, charity, and penance to the gods.'

" 'Wealth, like a tree, grows from a tiny seed. The first copper you save is the seed from which your tree of wealth shall grow. The sooner you plant that seed, the sooner shall the tree grow. And the more faithfully you nourish and water that tree with consistent savings, the sooner you may bask in contentment beneath its shade.' So saying this, ze took the tablets and walked away."

Arkad continued, "I thought much about what the old person had said to me, and it seemed reasonable. So, I decided that I would try it. Each time I was paid I took one from each ten pieces of copper and hid it away. And strange as it may seem, I was no shorter of funds than before. I noticed little difference as I managed to get along without it. But often I was tempted, as my savings began to grow, to spend it on some of the good things the merchants displayed, brought by camels and ships from the land of the Phoenicians. But I wisely refrained.

"On the twelfth month after Algamish left, ze returned and said to me,

" 'Child, have you paid yourself not less than one-tenth of all you have earned for the past year?'

"I answered proudly, 'Yes, master, I have.'

" 'This is good,' was the beaming response, 'and what have you done with it?'

" 'I have given it to Azmur, the brick maker, who told me ze was traveling across the far seas and in Tyre. Ze would buy for me the rare jewels of the Phoenicians. When Azmur returns, we shall sell these at high prices and divide the earnings.'

" 'Every fool must learn,' Algamish growled, '*but why trust the knowledge of a brick maker about jewels? Would you go to the bread maker to inquire about the stars? No, by my tunic, you would go to the astrologer, if you had the power to think*. Your savings are gone, youth; you have jerked your wealth tree up by the roots. But plant another. Try again. And next time, if you would seek advice about jewels, go to the jewel merchant. If you seek to know the truth about sheep, go to the shepherd. Advice is one thing that is freely given away, but watch that you take only what is worth having. *The person who takes advice about their savings from one who is inexperienced in such matters, shall pay with zir savings for proving the falsity of their opinions*.' Saying this, the wise person went away."

Arkad looked to the side and cleared zir throat, "And it was as Algamish said. 'The Phoenicians were scoundrels, what they sold to Azmur were worthless bits of glass that looked like gems. But as Algamish had bid me, I again saved each tenth copper. For I had formed the habit, it was no longer difficult.

"Again, twelve months later, Algamish came to the room of the scribes and addressed me. 'Pray tell, what progress have you made since I last saw you?'

" 'I have paid myself faithfully, and my savings I have entrusted to Agger, the shield maker, to buy bronze. Each fourth of the month ze pays me rent.'

"A subtle smile crossed Algamish's face. 'That is good. And what do you do with the rental?'

" 'I hold a great feast with honey and fine wine and spiced cake. Also, I have bought myself a scarlet tunic. And some day, I too shall buy myself a young camel upon which to ride.'

"To which Algamish laughed and said, 'You do eat the children of your savings. Then how do you expect your coin to work for you? And how can it have children that will also work for you? First, build an army of golden bonded servants and then many a rich banquet may you enjoy without regret.' So saying this, the wise person left once more.

"Nor did I see Algamish again for two years. When ze once again returned, zir face was full of deep lines and zir eyes drooped—for ze was growing old. 'Arkad, has thou yet achieved the wealth thou dreamed of? And do you still take the advice of brick makers?' ze asked.

" 'About brick making they give good advice.' I retorted with a smile.

" 'And what do you do with these coins thou earned?'

" 'I still buy bronze from Agger, the shield maker. Yet, ze cannot work as much bronze as I wish to buy, and the other shield makers are scoundrels. So, I have entrusted my coins to a wise money lender, who has known the shepherds for many years. Ze lends small loans to the sheep merchants beyond the gates, so they may buy the good flocks and take them into the city to be sold.'

"Algamish smiled and took a moment before responding. 'Arkad,' the wise person continued, 'you have learned your lessons well. You first learned to live upon less than you could earn. Then you learned to seek advice from those who were competent through their own experiences in the matters at hand. And, lastly, you have learned to make gold work for you. You have taught yourself how to acquire money, how to keep it, and how to use it. Therefore, you are competent for a responsible position.

" 'I am becoming an old person. My children think only of spending and give no thought to earning. My interests are so great and I fear they are too much for me to look after in my long years. If you go to Nippur and look after my lands there, I shall make you my partner and you shall share in my estate."

A wave of contentment washed over Arkad's face, "So I went to Nippur and took charge of Algamish's holdings, which were large. And because I was full of ambition and I had already mastered the three laws of successfully handling wealth, I was able to greatly increase the value of the properties. So, I prospered much and when the spirit of Algamish departed for the Land of the Darkness, I did share in their estate as ze had arranged under the law," so spoke Arkad.

When Arkad had finished the tale, one of the friends said, "You were indeed fortunate that Algamish made you an heir."

Arkad quickly retorted, "Fortunate only in that I had the desire to prosper before I first met Algamish. For four years did I not prove my definiteness of purpose by keeping one-tenth of all I earned? Would you call a fisherfolk lucky, who, for years, studied the habits of the fish so that with each changing wind, ze could cast their nets at them? Opportunity is a haughty god who wastes no time with those who are unprepared."

"Willpower!" barked Arkad. "What nonsense. Do you think willpower gives a person the strength to lift a burden the camel cannot carry, or to draw a load the oxen cannot budge? Willpower is but the unflinching purpose to carry out a task you set for yourself to fulfill. If I set for myself a task, be it ever so trifling, I shall see it through. How else shall I have confidence in myself to do important things?

"Should I say to myself, 'For a hundred days as I walk across the bridge into the city, I will pick from the road a pebble and cast it into the stream,' and do it? If on the seventh day I passed by without remembering, I would not say to myself, 'Tomorrow I will cast two pebbles which will do as well.' Instead, I would retrace my steps and cast the pebble.

"Not on the twentieth day would I say to myself, 'Arkad, this is useless. What does it avail you to cast a pebble every day? Throw in a handful and be done with it.' No, I would not say that, nor would I act on it. When I set a task for myself, I complete it. Therefore, I am careful not to start tasks that are impractical, for I also love my leisure."

And then another friend spoke up and said, "If what you tell is true, and it does seem, as you have said, reasonable, then being so simple, if all people do it, there will not be enough wealth to go around."

"Wealth grows wherever people exert energy," Arkad replied. "If a rich person builds themself a new palace, is the gold ze pays out gone? No, the brick maker has part of it and the laborer has part of it, and the artist has part of it. And everyone who labors upon the house has part of it. Yet, when the palace is completed, is it not worth all its costs? Is the ground upon which it stands not worth more because the palace is there? And is the adjoining ground not worth more as well? Wealth grows in magical ways. No person can predict the limit of it. Have the Phoenicians not built great cities on barren coasts with the wealth that comes from their ships of commerce upon the seas?"

"What then do you advise us to do so that we also may become rich?" asked yet another of the group of friends. "The years have passed and we are no longer young people, yet we still have saved none."

"I advise that you take the wisdom of Algamish and say to yourselves, 'A part of all I earn is mine to keep.' Say it in the morning when you first arise. Say it at noon. Say it at night. Say it at every hour of the day. Say it to yourself until the words stand out like letters of fire across the sky. Impress yourself with the idea. Fill yourself with the thought. Then take whatever portion seems wise. Let it be not less than one-tenth and lay it by. Arrange your other expenditures to do this if necessary. But lay by that portion first. Soon, you shall realize the true joy of owning a treasure upon which you alone have the right to claim. As it grows, it will inspire you. A new greatness of life will thrill you.

"Greater efforts over time will lead to greater gains. When your earnings increase, will not the same percentage also be yours to keep? *Then learn to make your treasure work for you. Make it your bonded servant. Make its children and its children's children work for you. Ensure an income for your future.* Look thou at the aged and forget not that in the days to come thou also will be numbered among them. Therefore, invest your treasure with great caution so that it be not lost. Excessive rates of return are deceitful sirens that sing only to lure the unwary upon the rocks of loss and remorse.

"Provide also so that your family shall be without want—should the gods call you to their realms. For such protection it is always possible to make small payments at regular intervals. Therefore, the prosperous person delays not in expectation of a large sum, becoming available for such a wise purpose.

"Counsel with a wise person. *Seek the advice of people whose daily work is handling money.* Let them save you from such an error as I myself made in entrusting my money to the judgment of Azmur, the brick maker. A small return, and a safe one, is far more desirable than risk.

"Enjoy life as well while you are here. Do not overstrain or try to save too much. If one-tenth of all you earn is as much as you can comfortably keep, then be content to keep this portion. Live according to your means but do not let yourself become miserly and afraid to spend. Life is good and life is rich—with worthwhile things to enjoy."

Arkad's friends gave their thanks and went along their ways. Some were silent because they had no imagination and could not understand zir wisdom. Some were sarcastic, believing that someone so rich should divide with old friends who are not so fortunate.

But a few had in their eyes a new light. They realized that Algamish had come back each time to the room of the scribes because ze was watching a person work their way out of darkness into light. When that person had found the light, a place awaited zir. No one could fill that place—until ze had for zirself worked out their own understanding—until they themselves were ready to seize the opportunity.

The latter were the ones who, in the following years, frequently revisited Arkad, who welcomed them gladly in return. Arkad counseled with them and gave freely of zir wisdom as people of broad experience were always glad to do so. Arkad went as far as guiding them in investing their savings wisely—bringing in a good interest with safety that would neither be lost nor entangled in ventures that paid no dividends.

The turning point in these people's lives had come upon that day when they realized the truth that had come from Algamish to Arkad and from Arkad to them.

"A part of all you earn is yours to keep."

ARKAD'S WISDOM

Parable 3

Sargon, the Great Ruler of the City

THE GLORY of Babylon endures. Across the ages, its reputation came to be as the richest of all cities, and its treasures just as fabulous. Yet, it was not always so. The riches of Babylon were the results of the wisdom of its people. They first had to learn how to become wealthy.

When the Great Ruler of the City, Sargon, returned to Babylon after defeating the enemies, Elamites, ze was confronted with a serious situation. The Royal Chancellor explained it to the Great Ruler of the City thus:

"The people seem unable to support themselves. After many years of great prosperity, brought to our people because Your Majesty built the great irrigation canals and the mighty temples to the gods, now that these works are completed. The laborers are without employment. The merchants have few customers. The farmers are unable to sell their harvest. The people do not have enough gold to buy food."

"But where has all the gold that we spent for these great improvements gone?" demanded the Ruler.

"It has found its way, I fear," responded the Chancellor, "into the possession of a few very rich citizens of our city. It filtered through the fingers of most of our people as quickly as the goat's milk that went through the strainer. Now that the stream of gold has ceased to flow, most of our people have nothing to do to make their earnings."

The Great Ruler of the City was thoughtful for some time. Then ze asked, "Why should so few people be able to acquire all the gold?"

"Because they know how to," replied the Chancellor. "One may not condemn a person for succeeding by knowledge. Neither may one justly take away from those who have earned their wealth fairly and give it to those people of lesser ability."

"But why," demanded the Ruler, "should not all the people learn how to accumulate gold and therefore become rich and prosperous themselves?"

The Chancellor replied, "Indeed it is quite possible, Your Majesty. But who can teach them? Certainly not the Holy People, for they know nothing of making money"

"Who knows best among the fine people of our grand city how to become wealthy, Chancellor?" asked the Good Ruler.

"Your question answers itself, Your Majesty. Who has amassed the greatest wealth in Babylon?"

"Well said, my able Chancellor. It is Arkad. Ze is the richest person in all of Babylon. Bring zir before me tomorrow."

***

The following day, as the Great Ruler of the City had decreed, Arkad appeared before zir, straight and sprightly despite living to see a hundred seasons.

"Arkad," spoke the Good Ruler of the city, "is it true thou are the richest person in Babylon?"

"It is as reported, Thy Majesty, and no person disputes it."

"How have thou become so wealthy?" asked the Chancellor.

"By taking advantage of opportunities available to all citizens of our good city."

"Thou had nothing to start with?" inquired the Ruler.

"Only a great desire for wealth. Besides this, nothing," Arkad humbly replied.

"Arkad," continued the Ruler, "our city is in a very unhappy state because while the majority of our citizens lack the knowledge to keep any part of the gold they receive, only a few people know how to acquire wealth and, therefore, monopolize it. It is my desire that Babylon be the wealthiest city in the world. Therefore, it must be a city of many wealthy citizens. Therefore, we must teach all the people how to acquire riches. Tell me, Arkad, is there any secret to acquiring wealth? Can it be taught?"

"It is practical, Thy Majesty. That which one person knows can be taught to others."

The Great Ruler of the City's eyes glowed. "Arkad, thou speak the words I wish to hear. Will thou lend thyself to this great cause? Will thou teach thy knowledge to schools for teachers, each of whom shall teach others until there are enough trained to teach these truths to every worthy subject in my domain?"

Arkad bowed and said, "I am thy humble servant to command. Whatever knowledge I possess, I shall gladly give for the betterment of my fellow citizens and the glory of the Great Ruler of the City. If I may be so bold, let your good Chancellor arrange for me a class of one hundred people and I will teach them those seven cures which did fatten my purse, for none was leaner than mine in all of Babylon."

***

A fortnight later, in compliance with the Ruler's command, the chosen hundred assembled in the great hall of the Temple of Learning, seated upon colorful rugs in a semicircle. Arkad sat beside a small table upon which smoke arose from a sacred lamp, sending forth a strange and pleasing odor that filled the room.

"Behold, the richest person in Babylon," whispered a student, nudging a neighbor as Arkad arose. "Arkad is but a person, even as the rest of us."

"As a loyal subject of our Great Ruler of the City," Arkad began, "I stand before you in zir command. Once, I was a poor youth who did greatly desire gold, and because I found knowledge that enabled me to acquire it. Ze asks that I impart my knowledge unto you."

"I began my fortune in the humblest of ways," Arkad continued. "I had no advantage that was not enjoyed as fully by you and every other citizen of Babylon. The first storehouse of my treasure was a well-purse. I loathed its useless emptiness. I desired it be round and full, clinking with the sound of gold. Therefore, I sought every remedy for a lean purse. I found seven.

"To you, who are assembled before me today, shall I explain the seven cures for a lean purse which I do recommend to all people who desire liberal amounts of coin. Every day for seven days will I explain to you one of these seven remedies.

"Listen attentively to the knowledge that I will impart. Debate my words with me. Discuss it among yourselves. Master these lessons thoroughly, so that you may also plant in your own purse the seed of wealth. First must each of you start wisely to build a fortune of your own. If you are competent, and only then, you will be ready to teach these truths to others.

"I shall teach you in simple ways how to fatten your purses. This is the first step leading to the Temple of Wealth, and no person may climb who cannot plant their feet firmly upon the first step. We shall now consider the first cure..."

START THY PURSE TO FATTENING

Parable 4

STANDING BEFORE THE CLASS, Arkad spoke to the thoughtful person in the second row, "My good friend, at what craft do thou work?"

"I," replied the person, "am a scribe and carve records upon the clay tablets."

"Even at such labor did I myself earn my first coppers. Therefore, thou have the same opportunity to build a fortune as I," Arkad then spoke to a florid-faced person on the farther back of the row. "Pray tell, what also does thou do to earn thy bread?"

"I am a meat butcher. I do buy the goats that the farmers raise and kill. Selling the meat to the house people and their hides to the sandal makers." the person responded.

"Because thou do also labor and earn, thou have every advantage to succeed what I did," in this way did Arkad proceed to find out how each person labored to earn their living. When ze had done questioning them, ze said:

"Now, my students, it may appear that there are many trades and labors at which people can earn coins. Each of the ways of earning is a stream of gold from which the worker diverts their labor a portion to their own purse. Therefore, into the purse of each of you flows a stream of coins large or small according to their ability. Is it not so?"

Thereupon they agreed that it was so.

"Then," continued Arkad, "if each of you desired to build for yourself a fortune, is it not wise to start by utilizing that source of wealth which you already have established?"

To this, they agreed.

Then Arkad turned to a humble person who had declared themself to be an egg merchant. "If thou select one of thy baskets and put into it each morning ten eggs and take out from it each evening but nine eggs, what will eventually happen?"

"It will become overflowing in time."

"Why?"

"Because each day I put in one more egg than I take out."

Arkad turned to the class with a smile. "Does any person here have a lean purse?"

First, they looked amused.

Then they laughed.

Finally, they waved their purses in jest.

"All right," ze continued, "now I shall tell thee the first remedy I learned to cure a lean purse. Do exactly as I have suggested to the egg merchant. For every ten coins put within thy purse, take out for use but nine. Thy purse will begin to fatten at once and its increasing weight will feel good in thy hand and bring satisfaction to thy soul."

"Do not discount this because of its simplicity. Truth is always simple. I told thee I would tell how I built my fortune. This was my beginning. I, too, carried a lean purse and cured it because there was naught enough coins within to satisfy my desires. But when I began to take out from my purse but nine parts of ten I put in, it began to fatten. As surely as the sun rises in the plains and sets in the hills, so shall thy purse fatten too."

"Now I will tell a strange truth, the reasons for which I do not know: when I ceased to pay out more than nine-tenths of my earnings, I managed to get along just as well. I was not shorter of coin than before. Also, before long, coins indeed came to me more easily than before. Surely it is a law of the gods that unto a person who keeps and spends not a certain part of all their earnings, shall gold come more easily."

"Likewise, for reasons I know not of a person whose purse is empty, gold does seem to avoid it." Arkad said solemnly.

"Which do you desire the most? Is it the gratification of thy desires of each day: a jewel, a bit of finery, better garments, more food; things quickly gone and forgotten? Or is it substantial belongings: gold, lands, herds, merchandise, income-bringing investment? *The coins taken from thy purse bring the first. The coins left within thy purse will bring the latter.*

This, my students, was the first cure I discovered for my lean purse: 'For each ten coins I put in, I spend but nine.' Debate this amongst yourselves. If any person proves it untrue, tell me upon the morrow when we shall meet again," so concluded the first day's lesson.

CONTROL THY EXPENDITURES

Parable 5

"**SOME OF OUR MEMBERS**, my students, have asked me this: 'How can a person keep one-tenth of all they earn in their purse when all the coins they earn are not enough for their necessary expenses?' "

So, on the second day, Arkad addressed this challenge.

Raising zir voice, Arkad began, "Yesterday, how many of thee in this great room carried a lean purse?"

"All of us," answered the class.

"Yet, all before me in this class do not earn the same. Some earn much more than others. Some have much larger families to support. Yet, all purses were equally lean. Now I will tell thee an unusual truth about people and the children of people. It is this; *That what each of us calls our 'necessary expenses' will always grow equal to our incomes unless we protest to the contrary.*"

"Confuse not the necessary expenses with thy desires. Each of you, together with your good families, have more desires than your earnings can gratify. Therefore, thy earnings are spent to gratify the desires insofar as they will go. Still though, thou retain many ungratified desires."

"All people are burdened with more desires than they can gratify. Because of my wealth do you think I may gratify every desire? 'Tis a false notion. There are limits to my time. There are limits

to my strength, my stamina. There are limits to the distance I may travel. There are limits to what I may eat. There are limits to the zest with which I may enjoy life."

"I now tell you that just as weeds grow in a field wherever the farmer leaves space for their roots, so do desires freely grow in people whenever there is a possibility of the desire being gratified. Thy desires are a multitude and those desires that may actually be gratified are but a few."

"Study thoughtfully your accustomed habits of living. Here within may be found certain accepted expenses that most often can be wisely reduced or eliminated. *Let thy motto be one hundred percent of the appreciated value demanded for each coin spent.*"

"Therefore, engrave upon the clay or sand each thing for which thou desire to spend. Select those that are necessary and others that are only possible through the expenditure of nine-tenths of your income. Cross out the rest—consider them a part of that great multitude of life's desires that must go unsatisfied and regret them not."

"Calculate the necessary expenses. Touch not the one-tenth that is fattening thy purse. Let this be thy great desire that is being fulfilled. Thy purpose in life shall be making thy purse fat. Keep working within thy budget. Keep adjusting it to help thyself. Make it thy first assistant in supporting thy fattening purse."

Hereupon one of the students, wearing a robe of red and gold, arose and said, "I am a free person. I believe that it is my right to enjoy the good things of life. Therefore, do I rebel against the bonded servantry of a budget which determines just how much I may spend and for what. I feel it would take much pleasure from my life and make me little more than a pack-ass to carry a burden."

To this free person, Arkad replied, "Who, my friend, would

determine thy budget?"

"I would make it for myself," responded the protesting one.

"In that case, if a donkey were to budget its burden, would it include their jewels and rugs and heavy bars of gold? Not so. The donkey would include hay, grain, and a bag of water for the desert trails. The purpose of a budget is to help thy purse fatten. It is to assist thee to have thy necessities and, insofar as attainable, thy other desires. It is to enable thee to realize thy most cherished desires by defending them from thy casual wishes. Like a bright candle in a dark cave, thy budget shows the leaks from thy purse and enables thee to stop them and control thy expenditures for definite and gratifying purposes.

This, then, is the second cure for a lean purse. 'Budget thy expenses that thou may have coins to pay for thy necessities, to pay for thy enjoyments and to gratify thy worthwhile desires without spending more than nine-tenths of thy earnings.' "

MAKE THY GOLD MULTIPLY

Parable 6

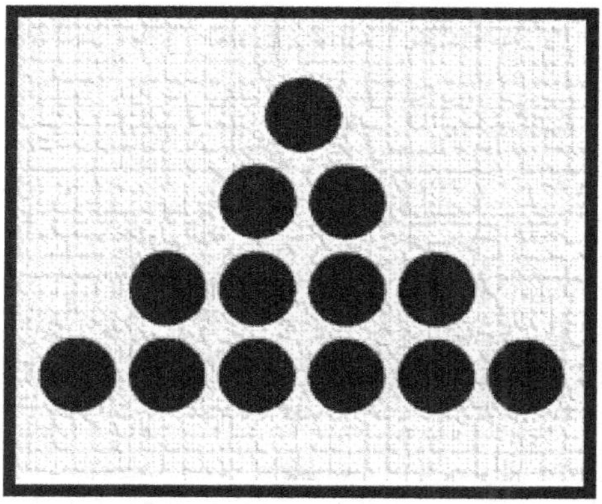

"**BEHOLD,** thy lean purse is fattening," so spoke Arkad upon the third day of class. "Thou have disciplined thyself to leave within one-tenth of all thou have earned. Thou have controlled thy expenditures to protect thy growing treasure."

"Next, we will consider means to put thy treasure to labor and to increase itself. Gold in a purse is gratifying to earn and satisfies a miserable soul but the truth is that it earns nothing. The gold we may retain from our earnings is only the start. The earnings it will make shall build our fortunes," spoke Arkad to the room.

"How, therefore, can we put our gold to work? My first investment was unfortunate, for I lost it all. Its tale I will share with you all later. However, my first profitable investment was a loan I made to a person named Agger, a shield maker. Once each year did ze buy large shipments of bronze, brought from across the sea to use in their trade. Lacking sufficient capital to pay the merchants, ze would borrow from those who had extra coins. Ze was an honorable person. A loan made to Agger would be repaid as assuredly as the sun rises on the plains in the morning. After borrowing, Agger would repay with a generous rental as the shields were sold.

"Each time I loaned to them, I also loaned back the rental Agger paid to me. Therefore, not only did my capital increase, but its earnings grew as well. Most gratifying was to have these sums returned to my purse with consistency.

"I tell you, my students, a person's wealth is not in the coins carried; it is the income a person builds. The golden stream that continually flows into their purse and keeps thy purse always bulging. That is what every person truly desires, whether or not they realize it. That is what each one of thee before me desires. An income that continues to come whether thou works or travels.

"Great income I have acquired. So great that I am called the richest person in our city. My loans to Agger were my first training in profitable investment. Gaining wisdom from this experience, I extended my loans and investments as my capital increased. From a few sources at first, then from many sources later on, coins flowed into my purse like a golden stream of wealth, available for such wise uses as I should decide.

"Behold from my humble earnings. I had accumulated a hoard of golden-bonded servants, each laboring without rest and earning yet more gold. As they labored for me, so did their children and their children's children also labored until great was the income from their combined efforts.

"Gold increases rapidly when making reasonable earnings as thou shalt see from the following:

"A farmer, when their first child was born, took ten pieces of silver to a money lender and asked them to keep the silver on rental until the farmer's eldest child became twenty years of age. This the money lender did, and agreed the rental should be one-fourth of its value every four years. The farmer asked, that because this sum is for their child and not for themself, the rental shall be added to the principal.

"When the eldest child had reached the ripe age of twenty years, the farmer again went to the money lender to inquire about the silver. The money lender explained that because this sum had been increased by compound interest, the original ten pieces of silver had now grown to thirty-and-one-half pieces.

"The farmer was well pleased and because the grown child did not need the coins, ze left the coins with the money lender. When the child itself grew to the ripest age of 50, with the parent meantime having passed to the other world, the money lender paid in settlement 167 pieces of silver.

"Thus in 50 years, the investment had multiplied itself at rental almost seventeen times.

"This, then, is the third cure for a lean purse: to put each coin to labor so that it may reproduce its kind. Like a fruit tree, growing from one fruit, to which, in time, a great tree with scores of fruits hanging off the branches will grow. *Even as the fields bloom and young and firm bodies become soft over time, thy golden stream of coins shall still flow with consistency into thy purse.*"

GUARD THY TREASURES FROM LOSS

Parable 7

"**MISFORTUNE LOVES** a shining mark." Arkad said on the fourth day of lectures. "Gold in a person's purse must be guarded with firmness, else it might be forever lost. Thus, it is wise that we first secure small amounts and learn to protect them before the gods can entrust us with larger sums."

"Every owner of gold is tempted by opportunities whereby it would seem that a person could make large sums by its investment in most plausible projects. Often friends and relatives are eager to enter such investments and urge others to follow."

"The first sound principle of investment is security for thy principal. As the sheep pastors say, 'trust in the gods… but tie up thy camel at night.' The penalty of risk is probable loss. Study carefully, before parting with thy treasure. Seek assurance that it may be safely reclaimed. Be not misled by thine own romantic desires to make wealth rapidly."

"Before it's loaned to any person, assure thyself of their ability to repay in full and their reputation for so. Thus, thou may not unwittingly be giving the receiver a present of thy hard-earned coin."

"Before entrusting thy gold as an investment in any field,

acquaint thyself with the dangers which may befall upon thy coin. My own first investment was a tragic experience. The guarded savings of a year's laboring, I entrusted to a brick maker, named Azmur, who was traveling over the far seas and in Tyre. Agreeing to buy for me the rare jewels of the Phoenicians. These we would sell upon their return and divide the profits."

"Alas, the Phoenicians were scoundrels and sold Azmur bits of glass. My treasure was lost. *Today, my training would show me at once the folly of entrusting a brick maker to buy jewels.*"

"Therefore, I do advise from the wisdom of my own experiences: do not be too confident of thy own wisdom in entrusting thy treasures to the possible pitfalls of investments. Better by far to consult the wisdom of those experienced in handling coin for profit. Such advice is freely given for the asking and may readily possess a value equal in gold to the sum thou consider investing. In truth, such is its actual value if it saves thee from loss."

Finishing the day's lesson, Arkad bellowed, "Just as the Great Ruler of the City has the citizens pay taxes each year for protection, so may one think of the value of this advice as being the sum of their investment. Put another way, *the tax for ignorance could be the sum of thy investment*. This, then, is the fourth cure for a lean purse and of great importance if this lesson prevents thy purse from being emptied once it has become well-filled.

"Guard thy treasure from loss by investing only where thy principal is safe, where it may be reclaimed if desirable, and where thou will not fail to collect a fair rental. *Consult with wise people with a history of success*. Secure the advice of those experienced in the profitable handling of gold. Let their wisdom protect thy treasure from unsafe investments."

MAKE OF THY DWELLING A PROFITABLE INVESTMENT

Parable 8

"**IF A PERSON** sets aside nine parts of their earnings upon which to live and enjoy life, and if any part of these nine parts a person can turn into a profitable investment without detriment to their wellbeing, then so much faster will their treasures grow," spoke Arkad to the class at their fifth day of lessons.

"Too often do many of the good citizens of Babylon raise their families in unseemly quarters. They pay, often to exacting landlords, liberal rentals for rooms where their spouses do not have a spot to raise the blooming flowers that brings bliss to a person's heart, and their children have no place to run and play their games except in the unclean alleys.

"No person's family can fully enjoy life unless they do have a plot of ground wherein children can play in the clean earth and where the spouse may raise not only trendy blossoms but good rich herbs to feed the family."

Continuing, Arkad said, "To a person's heart, it brings gladness to eat the figs from their own trees and the grapes of their own vines. To own their domicile and to have a place they are proud to care for puts confidence in their heart and greater effort behind all their endeavors. Therefore, I recommend that every person owns the roof that shelters them."

"Nor is it beyond the ability of any well-intentioned person to own their home. Has not our Great Ruler of the City so widely extended the walls of Babylon that much land is now unused and may be purchased at sums most reasonable?"

"Also I say to you, my students, that the money lenders gladly consider the desires of people who seek homes and land for their families. Thou may readily borrow to pay the brick maker and the builder for such commendable purposes, if thou can show a reasonable portion of the necessary sum which thou thyself provided," said Arkad.

"Then, when the house is built, thou can pay the money lender with the same regularity as thou did pay the landlord. Because each payment will reduce thy indebtedness to the money lender, a couple decades will satisfy their loan. Then thy heart will be glad because thou will own thy own right a valuable property and thy only cost will be the Great Ruler of the City's humble taxes."

"Furthermore, will thy good spouse go more often to the river to wash thy robes, each time returning with a goatskin of water to pour upon the growing things."

"Be wary though, because a dwelling would only cost a person who cannot make it profitable. Devise ways to make thy land a home and a rental. Rather it be by growing those herbs which do fetch a fair price at market or by renting out a portion of thy sanctuary. *If this critical step is not taken, this home will just provide additional costs for which a humble person must pay.* To truly live life with great liberality, be wise and make it so thou do not even pay a shekel for a spot to rest thy head for the long nights."

Summarizing, Arkad said: "Thus, there come many blessings to the person who owns their own house. And greatly will it reduce their cost of living, making available more of their earnings for pleasures and the gratification of their desires. This, then, is the fifth cure for a lean purse: own thy own home."

ENSURE A FUTURE INCOME

Parable 9

“**THE LIFE OF EVERY PERSON** proceeds from childhood to old age,” so addressed Arkad to the class upon the sixth day. “This is the path of life, and no person may deviate from it unless the gods call on them prematurely to the Land of the Darkness. Therefore, do I say that it behooves a person to make preparations for a suitable income for the days to come when they are no longer young.”

“In thy case, make preparations for thy family should they be no longer with them to comfort and support them. This lesson shall instruct thee in providing a full purse when time has made thee less able to earn.”

“The person who, through their understanding of the laws of wealth, acquires a growing surplus of such coins, should give thought to those future days. A wise person should plan out certain investments or provisions that may endure safely for many years yet will be available when the time arrives for which they have so wisely anticipated.”

“There are diverse ways by which a person may provide safety for their future. They may provide a hiding place and within bury a secret hoard of coin. Yet, no matter how skillfully it is hidden, it may still become the loot of thieves. For this reason, I recommend a different plan.”

“A person may buy houses or lands for this purpose. If wisely chosen as to their usefulness and value in the future, they are permanent in their value and their earnings or their sales will provide well for this purpose. Keep in mind, places like islands or parcels within the walls of a great city may have a limited plot of land. It seems like more and more people are born each year. This can increase the value thy property as land grows scarce and demand rises."

"A person may loan a small sum to the money lender and increase it at regular periods. The rental which the money lender adds to this will largely add to its increase."

"I do know of a sandal maker, named Ansan, who explained to me not long ago that each week, for eight years, ze had deposited with the money lender just two pieces of silver. The money lender had recently provided Ansan an accounting over which ze gladly rejoiced. The total of their small deposits with the rental at the customary rate of one fourth of their value for each four years, had now become 1042 pieces of silver."

"I did gladly encourage Asan further by demonstrating, with my knowledge of the numbers, that in 12 years more, if ze would keep adding regular deposits of two pieces of silver each week, the money lender would owe Ansan 4,000 pieces of silver, a worthy compensation for the rest of Ansan's life!"

"Surely, when such a small payment made with regularity does produce such profitable results, no person can afford not to insure a treasure for their old age and the protection of their family, regardless of how prosperous their business and their investments may be."

"I think that I might say more about this... In my mind rests a belief that someday, wise people will devise a plan to insure against the loss of a family's wealth against the death of the bread earner. In such a system, whereby many people pay in but a trifling sum regularly, the aggregate makes a handsome sum for the family of each member who passes to the Land of

Darkness. This I see as something desirable and which I would highly recommend."

"But, today it is not possible as it must reach beyond the life of any person or any partnership to operate. It must be as stable as the Great Ruler of the City's throne. I feel that such a plan shall come to pass one day and it will be a great blessing to many people, because even the first small payment would secure a snug fortune for the family if a member's passing takes place."

"But because we live in our own day and not in the days which are to come, we must take advantage of those means and ways of accomplishing our purposes. Therefore, I urge all people, that they, by wise and well-thought-out methods, do provide against a lean purse in their mature years. For a lean purse to a person no longer able to earn or to a family without its head is a great tragedy."

"This, then, is the sixth cure for a lean purse. Provide in advance for the needs of thy growing age and the protection of thy family."

INCREASE THY ABILITY TO EARN

Parable 10

"**THIS DAY I SPEAK TO THEE**, my students, one of the most vital remedies for a lean purse. Yet, I will talk not of gold but of yourselves, of the people beneath the robes of many colors who sit before me. I will talk to you of those things within the minds and lives of people which do work for or against the success we all desire," so did Arkad address the class on the seventh day.

"Not long ago a young person came to me seeking to borrow money. When I questioned them about the cause of this necessity, they complained that their earnings were insufficient to pay their expenses. Thereupon I explained to them that, with this being the case, ze was a poor customer for the money lender, as they possessed no surplus earning capacity to repay the loan.

" 'What thou need,' I told this young person, 'Is to earn more coins. What tasks do thou do to increase thy capacity to earn?'

" 'All that I can do,' was the reply, 'six times within two moons have I approached my master to request my pay be increased, but without success. No person can ask more often than that.'

"We may smile at their simplicity, yet ze did possess one of the vital requirements to increase their earnings. Within zir was a fervent desire to earn more money—a proper and commendable desire.

"Before any accomplishment can occur, there must be a specific desire. Thy desires must be strong and definite. General desires are

but weak longings. For a person to wish to be rich is of little purpose. For a person to desire five pieces of gold is a tangible desire for which a person can press to fulfillment. After ze has backed their desire for five pieces of gold with strength of purpose to secure it, ze can then find similar ways to obtain 10 pieces, and then 20, and later a thousand, and, behold, ze has become a wealthy person! In learning to secure this one definite small desire, ze has trained to secure a larger one. This is the process by which wealth is accumulated. First in small sums, then in larger amounts as a person learns and becomes more capable.

"Desires must be simple and definite. They defeat their own purpose should they be too many, too confusing, or beyond a person's training to accomplish.

"When a person perfects themselves in their calling, their ability to earn increases as well. Those days when I was a humble scribe carving upon the clay for a few coppers each day, I observed that other workers did more than I and were paid more. Therefore, did I determine that I would be exceeded by none. Nor did it take long for me to discover the reasons for their greater success. More interest in my work, more concentration upon my task, more persistence in my efforts, and behold, few people could carve more tablets in a day than I. With reasonable promptness, my increased skill was rewarded, nor was it necessary for me to go six times to my master to request recognition.

"The more wisdom we know, the more we may earn. That person who seeks to learn more of their craft shall be richly rewarded. If they are an artisan, they may seek to learn the methods and the tools of those most skillful in the same line. If they work at the law or at healing, they may consult and exchange knowledge with others of their calling. If they are merchants, they may continually seek better goods that can be purchased at lower prices."

***

"Always the affairs of people change and improve because keen-minded people seek greater skills so that they may better serve those upon whose patronage they depend. Therefore, I urge all people to be in the front rank of progress and not to stand still, lest they be left behind. Many things come to make a person's life rich with gainful experiences. Such things as the following, a person must do if they respect themselves.

"One must pay their debts with all the promptness within their power, refraining from purchasing that for which they are unable to pay.

"One must take care of their family so that they may think and speak well of them.

"One must create a will of record, so that in the case the gods call for them, a proper and honorable division of their property can be accomplished.

"One must have compassion upon those who are injured and befallen by misfortune and aid them within reasonable limits. They must do deeds of thoughtfulness to those dear to them."

***

"Thus, the seventh and last remedy for a lean purse is to cultivate thy own powers, to study and become wiser, to become more skillful, to act in a way that respects thyself. Thereby thou shall acquire confidence within thyself to achieve thy carefully considered desires.

"These, then, are the seven cures for a lean purse, which I urge upon all people who desire wealth, drawn from the experience of a long and successful life. *My students, there is more gold in Babylon than in thy wildest dreams. There is abundance for all.*

"Go forth and practice these truths so thou may prosper and

grow wealthy, as it is thy right." Arkad paused and looked over the whole class for a moment, as if appraising a fine camel freshly purchased. With a grin of appreciation, ze said, "Now, go forth and teach these truths so that every honorable subject of this great city may also share liberally in the ample wealth of our beloved people."

MEET THE GOD OF GOOD LUCK

Parable 11

"If a person be lucky, there is no foretelling of the possible extent of the good fortune that is about to come their way. Pitch zir into the Euphrates; and like as not, ze will swim out with a pearl in hand."

— Babylonian Proverb

THE DESIRE to be lucky was universal. It was just as strong in the chest of humans four thousand years ago in ancient Babylon as it was in the hearts of people today. They all hoped to be favored by the whimsical God of Good Luck.

Was there some way people could meet and attract this divine being? Not only in this god's favorable attention, but their generosity as well? Was there a way to attract good luck?

That was just what ancient Babylonians wished to know. Thus, it was exactly what they decided to discover. They were shrewd people and keen thinkers. That would explain why their city became the richest and most powerful city of their time.

In the distant past, they had no schools or colleges. Education was not as systematic as it is today; rather, it was acquired through a desire to learn and experience. Nevertheless, they had a center of learning, and a very practical one on top of that. Among the towered buildings in Babylon was one that ranked in importance with the palace of the Great Ruler of the City, the Hanging Gardens, and the Temples of the Gods. One would find scant mention of it in history books, or more likely no mention at all. And yet, it exerted a powerful influence upon the thought of that time.

This building was the Temple of Learning where the wisdom of the past was expounded by voluntary teachers and where subjects of popular interest were discussed in open forums. Within its walls, all people met as equals. The humblest of bonded servants could, with impunity, dispute the opinions of a prince of the royal house.

***

Among the many who frequented the Temple of Learning was Arkad. Ze alone had a special hall, where most evenings a large group of citizens—some old, some young, but mostly middle-aged, gathered to discuss and argue various interesting subjects. One particular evening, the subject was whether one knew how to attract good luck.

The sun had just set, like a great red ball of fire shining through the haze of desert dust, when Arkad strolled to zir accustomed platform. The hall was already full, a score of people were waiting for Arkad's arrival.

Addressing the people in the room, Arkad inquired, "What shall we discuss this evening?"

After a brief hesitation, a tall cloth weaver arose, as per custom, and addressed the teacher, "I have a subject I like to hear discussed yet hesitate to offer, lest it seems ridiculous to you, Arkad, and to my good friends here."

Upon being encouraged to offer it, both by Arkad and by calls from the others, the weaver continued.

"This day I have been lucky," the weaver said, "for I have found a purse in which there are pieces of gold. To continue to be lucky is my great desire, and I believe that all people share this desire as I do. So I propose we discuss how to attract good luck and perhaps discover ways on how it can be enticed to an individual."

"A most interesting subject has been raised," Arkad commented, "One worthy of our discussion. To some people, good luck is but a chance happening that, like an accident, may befall one without purpose or reason. Others do believe that the instigator of all good fortune is our most bounteous god, the God of Good Fortune. Ever anxious to reward with generous gifts those who are pleasing to their all-seeing eyes. Speak up, my friends. What say ye? Shall we seek to find if there are means by which good luck may be enticed to visit each and all of us?"

"Yes! Yes! Here, and much of it!" responded the growing group of eager listeners.

Thereupon Arkad continued, "To start our discussion, let us first hear from those among us who have enjoyed experiences similar to that of the cloth weaver in finding or receiving, without effort upon their part, valuable treasures or jewels."

There was a pause in which all looked about one another, expecting someone to reply but no one did.

"What? No one?" Arkad challenged. "Then this kind of luck must be rare indeed. Who, then, will offer a suggestion as to where we shall continue our search?"

"That, I will do," spoke a well-robed young citizen, rising. "When a person speaks or thinks of luck, is it not natural that the thoughts turn to the gaming tables? Is it not there, where we may find many people, courting the favor of the God of Good Fortune. Hoping that the gambler will be blessed with rich winnings?"

"Do not stop! Continue thy story!" a person interjected from the audience. "Tell us, did thou find favor with the God of Good Fortune at the gaming table? Did they assist thee by turning the cubes with the red side up, so thou filled thy purse at the dealer's expense? Or did they permit the blue sides to come up so the dealer raked in thy hard-earned coin?"

The young citizen joined the good-natured laughter, then replied, "I am not averse to admitting that the good god seemed not to know that I was even there. But how about the rest of you? Have you found this God of Good Fortune waiting about such places to roll the cubes, in your favor? If so, we are eager to hear as well as to learn."

"A wise start," broke in Arkad. "We meet here to consider all sides of each question. To ignore the gaming table would be to overlook an instinct common to most people: the love of taking chances with a small amount of silver in the hopes of winning a lot of gold."

"That one does remind me of the races yesterday," called out another listener. "If the gods frequent the gaming tables, certainly they do not overlook the races where the gilded chariots and the foaming horses offer far more excitement. Tell us honestly, Arkad, did the good god whisper to thee to place thy bet upon those gray horses from Nineveh yesterday? I was standing just behind thee and could scarcely believe my ears when I heard thee place a bet upon the gray ones. Thou knowest as well as any of us that no team in all Assyria can beat our beloved bays in a fair race."

"And yet, the good god must have nudged their hand ever so slightly. For at the last turn, the inside black stumbled and so interfered with our beloved bays so that the grays would win the race and score an unearned victory."

Arkad smiled indulgently at the banter. "What reason do we have to think that a good god would take that much interest in any person's mere bet upon the horses? To me the gods are full of love and dignity, for whose pleasure is to aid those who are in need and to reward those who are deserving. I look to find these gods, not at the gaming tables or the races where a person may lose more gold than they win, but in other places where the doings of people are more worthwhile and more worthy of reward.

"In tilling the soil, in honest trading, in all of human labor, there is an opportunity to make a profit upon these efforts and transactions. Perhaps not all the time a person will be rewarded, for sometimes, a person's judgement may be faulty, and other times the winds and the weather may defeat a person's most noble of efforts. Yet, if persistence abounds, one may expect a return of profit. This is because the chances of profit are always in their favor.

"But, when a person gambles, the situation is reversed. For the chances of profit are always against them and always in favor of the game keeper. My words are not a mere exaggeration, the luck of such games are fixed that it will always favor the keeper. It is a business in which people plan to make a liberal profit from the coins bet by the players. Few players realize how certain the keeper's gains are compared to their own uncertain chances of winning more than a trifling sum.

"For example, let us consider wagers placed upon the cube. Each time it is cast, we bet which side will be the uppermost. If it is the red side, the game master pays us four times our bet. But if any other of the five sides come uppermost, we lose our bet. Thus, the figures show that for each cast we have five chances to lose, but because the red pays four to one, we have but four chances to win. *In a night's play, the game master can expect to keep for themselves one-fifth of all the coins wagered.* Now, tell me, can a person expect to win more than occasionally when the odds are so arranged that the player should lose one-fifth of all their bets?"

"Yet, some people do win large sums at times," volunteered one of the listeners in a green robe.

"Quite so, they do," Arkad continued. "Realizing this, a question comes to me, whether money secured in such ways brings permanent value to those who are lucky. Among my acquaintances are many of the successful people of Babylon, yet I am unable to name a person whose success started from such a source. I know of none who began their fortune at the gaming tables.

"You who are gathered here tonight know many more of our substantial citizens than I shall ever know. To me, it would be of much interest to learn how many of our successful citizens can credit the gaming tables with their start to success. Suppose each of you tells of those you know. What say you?"

After a prolonged silence, a frail youth ventured, "Would thy inquiry include the game keepers?"

"If you can think of no other person," Arkad responded. "And not one of you can think of anyone else, then how about thyselves? Are there any consistent winners with us who hesitate to advise such a source for their incomes?"

A series of groans from the rear answered this challenge and spread amid much laughter.

"It would seem we are not seeking good luck in such places that the gods frequent," Arkad continued once the merriment died down. "Therefore, let us explore other fields. We have not found it in picking up lost wallets. Neither have we found it in haunting the gaming tables. As to the races, I must confess to having lost far more coins than I have ever gained."

After taking the measure of the class, Arkad began. "Now,

suppose we consider our trades and businesses. Is it not natural, after we conclude a profitable transaction, to consider the profits not good luck but a just reward for our efforts? I am inclined to think we may be overlooking the gifts of the gods. Perhaps they really do assist us when we do not appreciate their generosity. Who can suggest further discussion?"

Thereupon an elderly merchant arose, smoothing out their genteel white robe. "With thy permission, most honorable Arkad and my friends, I offer a suggestion. If, as you have said, we should take credit for our own industry and ability for our business success, then why not also consider the successes we almost enjoyed, but which escaped us, events which would have been more profitable? They would have been rare examples of good luck if they had actually happened. And because they were not brought to fulfilment, we cannot consider them as our just rewards. Surely, many people here have such experiences to relate to."

"That is a wise approach," Arkad approved. "Who among ye have had good luck within thy grasp only to see it escape?"

Many hands were raised, and a low murmur could be heard. Among them was that of the merchant. Arkad motioned to zir to speak. "As thou suggested this approach, we would like to hear first from thee," Arkad said.

"I will gladly relate a tale that illustrates how closely a person may approach good luck and how blindly ze may permit it to escape, much to their loss and later regret," the merchant said. "My name is Nurval, of Market Street.

"Many years ago, when I was a young person, newly married and well started to earn, my parent did come by one day and urged most strongly that I enter into an investment. One of my parent's good friend's children, Bau, had taken notice of a barren tract of land not far beyond the outer walls of our city. This land lay high above the canal where no water could reach it.

"Bau devised a plan to purchase this land and build three large water wheels that could be operated by oxen and thereby raise the life-giving water to the fertile soil. Once this was accomplished, Bau planned to divide the land into small tracts and sell them to the residents of the city for herb patches.

"Bau did not possess sufficient gold to complete such an undertaking. Like myself, Bau was a young person earning a fair sum. Bau's family, like mine, was large and of small means. Therefore, Bau decided to entice a group of people to enter the enterprise with them. The group was to be made up of twelve individuals, each of whom must be a money earner and agree to pay one-tenth of their earnings into the enterprise until the land was made ready for sale. All would then share justly in the profits, in proportion to their investment.

" 'My child, Nurval,' bespoke my parent unto me, 'thou are now in thy young personhood. It is my deep desire that thou begin the building of a valuable estate for thyself and that thou may become a respected citizen of our great city. I desire to see thee profit from a knowledge of the thoughtless mistakes of myself.'

"I then remarked, 'This, do I most ardently desire, my dear parent.'

" 'Then, I advise thee, Nurval,' continued my parent. 'My dear child, do what I should have done at thy age. From your earnings keep out one-tenth to put into a favorable investment. With this one-tenth of your earnings, it shall also earn, thou can by then, accumulate for thyself a valuable estate before thou reach my age.'

" 'Thy words are words of wisdom,' replied I. 'Greatly do I desire riches. Yet, there are many uses to which my earnings are called. Therefore, do I hesitate to do as thou advise. I am still just a young person. There is plenty of time.'

" 'So, I thought at thy age, yet behold, many years have passed and I have not yet made the beginning of the prosperity I yearn for your future,' responded my parent.

"To which I replied, 'We live in a different age, my wise parent. I shall avoid thy mistake.'

"My parent's face settled into a look of determination and said, 'Opportunity stands before thee, my child. It is offering a chance that may lead to wealth. I beg of thee, do not delay. Go upon the morrow to the child of my friend and bargain with them to pay ten percent of thy earnings into this investment. Go promptly upon the morrow. Opportunity waits for no one. Today it is here; soon it is gone. Therefore, delay not!'

"In spite of the advice of my parent, I did hesitate. There were beautiful new robes just brought by the tradesperson from the East. Robes of such richness and beauty my good partner and I felt we must each possess one. Should I agree to pay one-tenth of my earnings into the enterprise, we must deprive ourselves of these and other pleasures we dearly desire. I delayed making a decision until it was too late, much to my subsequent regret. The enterprise did prove to be more profitable than any person had prophesied. This is my tale, showing how I did permit good luck to escape."

Another listener, a swarthy person of the desert, broke in, "In this tale we see how luck waits to come to that person who accepts opportunity. To the building of an estate, there must always be a beginning. That start may be a few pieces of gold or silver, which a person diverts from their earnings to make a first investment. I, myself, am the owner of many herds. The start of my herds did begin when I was a mere child and did purchase with one piece of silver a young calf. This, being the beginning of my wealth, was of great importance to me.

"To take this first step toward building an estate is as good a stroke of luck as any person can come by. With all people, that first step, which changes them from a person who earns from their own labor to a person who draws dividends from the earnings of their gold, is important. Some, fortunately, take it when they are young and thereby outstrip in financial success. But still, there are also those who take it later and ones who are unfortunate, like the parent of this merchant, who never took it to begin with.

"Had our friend, the merchant, taken this step in their early life, when this opportunity came to them, this day they could be blessed with much more of this world's pleasures. Should the good luck of our friend, the cloth weaver, cause them to take such a step at this time, it will indeed be the beginning of much greater good fortune."

"Thank you! I would like to speak also," a stranger from another country said, arising. "I am a Syrian. Not well do I speak the tongue. I wish to call this friend—the merchant, Nurval... Maybe you think it is not polite, this name. Yet, I wish to call zir this and mean it with respect. But, alas, I do not know your words for it and if I do call it in Syrian, I am afraid that you will not understand. Therefore, please, some good, gentle person, tell me the right name that you call a person who puts off doing those things that might be good for zir."

"Procrastinator," called a voice.

"That person!" shouted the Syrian, waving hands excitedly, "Ze accepts no opportunity when it comes. Ze waits. Saying I have much business to do right now. By and by, I talk to thy morrow. But opportunity will not wait for such a slow one. The gods think if a person desires to be lucky, ze will step quickly. Any person who longs for success but does not act immediately when opportunity comes is a big procrastinator like our friend here, Nurval the merchant."

The merchant arose and bowed good-naturedly in response to the laughter. "My admiration to thee, stranger within our gates, who hesitates not to speak the truth to all who can hear."

"And now let us hear another tale of opportunity. Who here has another experience for us?" asked Arkad to the class.

"I have," responded a red-robed person of middle age. "I am a buyer of animals, mostly camels and horses. Sometimes I do also buy the sheep and goats. The tale I am about to relate will tell truthfully how opportunity came one night when I least expected it. Perhaps for this reason I did let it escape. Of this, you shall be the judge.

"Returning to the city one evening after a disheartening ten-day journey in search of the camels, I was much angered to find the gates of the city closed and locked. While my bonded servants spread our tent for the night, which we looked to spend with little food and no water, I was approached by an elderly farmer who, like ourselves, found themselves locked outside.

"The farmer approached me and began, 'Honored person, from thy appearance, I do judge thee to be a buyer. If this be so, I would like to sell to thee the most excellent flock of sheep I have just driven up. Alas, my good spouse lies very sick with a fever. I must return home in all haste. Buy my sheep so that I and my bonded servants may mount our camels and travel back without delay.'

"So dark it was that I could not see their flock, but from the bleating I did know it must be a large one.

"Having wasted ten days searching for camels I could not find, I was glad to bargain with the farmer. In zir anxiety, a most reasonable price was set. I accepted, knowing well my bonded servants could drive the flock through the city gates in the morning and sell at a substantial profit.

"With the bargain concluded, I called my bonded servants to bring torches so that we might count the flock which the farmer declared to count nine hundred. I shall not burden you, my fellow students, with a description of our difficulty in attempting to count so many thirsty, restless, milling sheep. It proved to be an impossible task. Therefore, I bluntly informed the farmer I would count them at daylight and pay by then.

"The farmer quickly responded, 'Please, most honorable person, pay me but two-thirds of the price tonight that I may be on my way. I will leave my most intelligent and educated bonded servant with you to assist and make the count in the morrow. This bonded servant is trustworthy and to them, thou can pay the balance.'

"But I was stubborn and refused to make payment that night. The next morning, before I awoke, the city gates opened and four buyers rushed out in search of flocks. They were most eager and willing to pay high prices because the city was threatened with siege and food was not plentiful. Nearly three times the price at which the farmer had offered the flock to me did the old farmer receive for it that morning. Such good luck I allowed to escape from my grasp that night."

"Here is a tale most unusual," commented Arkad. "What wisdom does it suggest?"

"The wisdom of making a payment immediately when we are convinced that our bargain is wise enough," suggested a venerable saddle maker. "If the bargain be good, then protection is needed against thy own weakness, as much as it is needed against any other person. We mortals are changeable, alas, I must say, it is more apt to change our minds when it is right than wrong. But we are stubborn indeed once it is wrong, and we are prone to vacillate and let opportunity escape when it is right.

My first judgement is often my best. Yet always have I found it difficult to compel myself to proceed with a good bargain when made. Therefore, as protection against my own weaknesses, I do make a prompt deposition thereon. This does save me from later regrets for the good luck that should have been mine."

"Thank you! Again, I wish to speak," said the Syrian, who was upon zir feet once more. "These tales are somehow made the same. Each opportunity flies away for a new reason. Each time, the gods come to a procrastinator, bringing good plans. Each time ze hesitates, not say, 'Right now best time, I do it quick.' How can ze succeed that way?"

"Wise are thy words, my foreign friend," responded the camel buyer. "Good luck fled from procrastination in both these tales. Yet, this is not unusual. The spirit of procrastination is within all people. We desire riches; yet, how often, when opportunity does appear before us, that the spirit of procrastination from within, urges various delays in our acceptance?"

"In listening to this spirit, we do become our own worst enemies. In my younger days, I did not know it by this long word our friend from Syria does enjoy. I did think at first it was my own poor judgment that caused me to lose many profitable trades. Later, I credited it to my stubborn disposition. At last, I did recognize it for what it was: a habit of needless delaying where action was required, prompt and decisive. How I hated it when its true character stood revealed. And with the bitterness of a wild ass hitched to a chariot, I did break loose from this enemy to my success."

"Thank you! I would like to ask a question to the wise merchant," the Syrian said. "You wear fine robes, not like those of poor people. You speak as a successful person. Tell us, do you listen now when procrastination whispers in your ear?"

"Like our friend the buyer, I also had to recognize and

conquer procrastination," responded the merchant. "*To me, it proved to be an enemy, ever watching and waiting to thwart my accomplishments.*

"The tale I did relate is but one of many similar instances I can tell to show how procrastination drove away my opportunities. 'Tis not difficult to conquer, once understood. No person willingly permits a thief to rob their bins of grain. Nor does any person willingly permit an enemy to drive away their customers and rob them of their profits. When I once recognized the acts my enemy was committing, I conquered them with determination. So must every person master their own spirit of procrastination before they can expect to share in the rich treasures of Babylon.

"What do you say, Arkad?" the Merchant continued. "Because you are the richest person in Babylon, many do proclaim you to be the luckiest. Do you agree with me that no person can arrive at a full measure of success until they have completely crushed the spirit of procrastination within themself?"

"It is even as thou say," Arkad admitted. "During my long life I have watched generation after generation, marching forward along these avenues of trade, science, and learning that lead to success in life. Opportunities come to all these people. Some grasped their chance and moved steadily to the gratification of their deepest desires, but the majority hesitated, faltered, and fell behind."

Arkad turned to the cloth weaver, "Thou did suggest that we debate good luck. Let us hear what thou now think upon the topic."

"I do see good luck in a different light," the weaver said. "I had thought of it as something most desirable that might happen to a person without effort upon their path. Now, I do realize such happenings are not the sort of thing one may attract to zirself. From our discussion I have come to learn that to attract good luck to oneself, it is necessary to take advantage of the opportunities. Therefore, in the future, I shall endeavor to make the best of such opportunities as they come to me."

"Thou have well grasped the truths brought forth in our discussion," Arkad replied. "Good luck, we do find, often follows opportunity but seldom comes otherwise. Our merchant friend would have found greater good luck had they accepted the opportunity the gods did present to them. Our friend, the buyer, likewise would have enjoyed good luck had ze completed the purchase of the flock and sold at such a handsome profit.

"We did pursue this discussion to find a means by which good luck could be enticed to us. I feel that we have found the way. Both the tales did illustrate how good luck follows opportunity. Here lies a truth that many similar tales of good luck, won or lost, could not change. The truth is this: *good luck can be enticed by being prepared for and then accepting opportunity*.

"Those eager to grasp opportunities for their betterment do attract the interest of the God of Good Fortune. This god is ever anxious to aid those who please themselves. People of action please them best.

"Action will lead ye forward to the successes ye do desire."

THOSE LAWS WHICH CAN'T BE DISPUTED

Parable 12

KALABAB WAS THE LEADER of a caravan. The people there were all carrying zir goods between the great wastelands of the desert from one city to another.

Earlier today, they found a beggar in the road. One of the caravan guards told zir to get out of the way. The beggar did not. The guard slapped zir, and Kalabab shouted "Stop!" and then told the guard to walk at the back of the caravan for the rest of the journey because of the shame the guard brought to them all.

Later that night, as tradition held, the caravan set up a great communal tent, where people would all tell stories around a small fire and drink dark tea.

One of the children, who did not yet know their manners, asked, "Kalabab, why did you let that smelly person walk with us? Shouldn't they be left to die? That is what they do outside the walls of Mesopotamia." Then the child's parents lightly slapped the little one and told them to speak only when spoken to.

Kalabab calmed the parent and said, "The youth's words are usually wise because they come from a place of truth and intrigue, rather than out of personal gain like many adults. I let the beggar walk with us because I, too, was once a beggar. Yet, I was fortunate enough to learn the five laws of gold, and I became successful like this."

The same kid, darting away from the mother who lunged toward them to stop them from talking again, spoke up, "You used to be smelly, too? How? You smell like expensive perfumes!"

With everyone laughing, Kalabab said, "Then let me tell ye all tonight, around the small communal fire, the five laws of gold."

***

"A bag heavy with gold or a clay tablet carved with words of wisdom," Kalabab said. "If ye had a choice, which would ye choose?"

By the flickering light from the fire of desert shrubs, the suntanned faces of the listeners, numbering twenty-seven, gleamed with interest.

"The gold, the gold," chorused the twenty-seven.

Old Kalabab smiled knowingly.

"Hmm," ze resumed, raising a hand. "Hear the wild dogs out there in the night. They howl and wail because they are lean with hunger. Yet feed them, and what do they do? They fight, they strut. Then fight and strut some more, giving no thought to the morrow that will surely come."

Kalabab drew zir white robe close to zir lean legs, for a cool night wind was blowing.

"It is just so with the children of people," Kalabab continued. "Give them a choice of gold and wisdom. What do they do? Ignore the wisdom and waste the gold. On the morrow they wail because they have no more gold. Gold is reserved for those who know its laws and abide by them.

"Because ye have served me faithfully upon our long journey, because ye cared well for my camels, because ye toiled uncomplainingly across the hot sands of the desert, and because ye fought bravely the robbers that sought to despoil my merchandise, I will tell ye this night the tale of the five laws of gold. Such a wise tale as ye never have heard before.

"Hark ye, with deep attention, to the words I speak, for if ye grasp their meaning and heed them, in the days that come, ye shall have much gold."

The confident Kalabab paused impressively. Above in a canopy of darkness with a hint of blue, the stars shone brightly in the crystal-clear skies of Babylon. Behind the group loomed their faded tents tightly stacked against possible desert storms. Beside the tents were neatly stacked bales of merchandise covered with skins. Nearby, the camel herd sprawled in the sand, some chewing their cuds contentedly, others snoring in hoarse discord.

"Thou have told us many good tales, Kalabab," spoke the chief packer. "We look to thy wisdom to guide us upon the morrow when our service with thee shall be at an end."

"I have but told ye of my adventures in strange and distant lands, but this night I shall tell ye of the wisdom of Arkad, the wise rich person."

"Much have we heard of zir," acknowledged the chief packer, "for Arkad was the richest person that ever lived in Babylon."

"The richest person indeed. For ze was wise in the ways of gold, even as no person had ever been beforehand. This night, I shall tell ye of zir great wisdom as it was told to me by Nomasir, Arkad's child, many years ago in Nineveh, when I was but a young one.

"My master and I had carried long into the night within the palace of Nomasir. I had helped my master bring great bundles of fine rugs, each one to be tried by Nomasir until zir choice of colors was satisfied. At last, ze was well pleased and commanded us to sit with them and drink a rare vintage of wine, odorous to thy nostrils yet unsettling to my stomach, which was unaccustomed to such a drink.

"Then, did Nomasir tell us this tale of the great wisdom of Arkad, from Nomasir's own lips, as I now shall tell it to ye."

***

"In Babylon," Kalabab began, "it is customary that the offspring of wealthy parents live with their elders in the expectation of inheriting the estate. Arkad did not approve of this custom. Therefore, when Nomasir reached a person's age of competence, Arkad said the following:

" 'My humble child, it is my desire that thou succeed to my estate. Thou must, however, first prove that thou are capable of wisely handling it. Therefore, I wish that thou go out into the world and show thy ability to acquire gold and to make thyself respected among people of good standing.

" 'To start thee well, I will give thee two things of which I, myself, was denied when I started as a poor youth to build up a mighty fortune.'

"Arkad continued, 'First, I give thee this bag of gold. If thou use it wisely, it will be the basis of thy future success. Second, I give thee this clay tablet upon which is carved the five laws of gold. If thou do but interpret these sacred laws in thine own actions, they shall bring thee competence and security.

" 'Ten years from this day, come back to the house of thy parent and give an account of thyself. If thou prove worthy, I will then make thee the heir to my estate.' Arkad then concluded zir instructions by saying, 'Otherwise, I will give it to the Holy People that they may barter for my soul via land consideration to the gods.' "

Kalabab continued relaying Nomasir's tale. "The ten years passed, and Nomasir, as agreed, returned to the house of zir wise parents who provided a great feast in honor of zir return, inviting many friends and relatives. After the feast was over, Arkad and zir partner mounted their shared throne-like seat at one wall of the great hall, and Nomasir stood before them to give an account of zirself, as was promised to Arkad.

"It was evening. The room was hazy with smoke from the wicks of the oil lamps that dimly lit it. Bonded servants in white woven jackets and tunics fanned the humid air rhythmically with long-stemmed palm leaves. A stately dignity colored the scene. The partner of Arkad and their two young offspring, with friends and other members of the family, sat upon the rugs before Nomasir, all eager listeners.

" 'My wise parent Arkad,' Nomasir began deferentially, 'I bow before thy wisdom. Ten years ago, when I stood at the gates of adulthood, thou bid me to go forth and become a person among people, instead of remaining a vassal to thy fortune.

" 'Thou gave me liberally of thy own gold. Thou gave me

liberally of thy great wisdom. Of the gold, alas! I must admit of a disastrous handling. It fled, indeed, from my inexperienced hands swiftly as a wild hare flees at the first opportunity from the youth who captured it.'

"Arkad smiled indulgently, 'Continue, Nomasir, thy tale interests me in all its details.'

" 'I decided to go to Nineveh,' Nomasir went on, 'as it was a growing city, believing that I might find there opportunities. I joined a caravan and, among its members, made numerous friends. Among these friends were two well-spoken people who had the most beautiful white horse I have seen and that they claimed was as swift as the wind.

" 'As we journeyed, they told me in confidence that in Nineveh was a wealthy person who owned a horse so swift that it had never been beaten. Its owner believed that no horse living could run with greater speed. Therefore, the owner would wager any sum, however large, that zir horse could outspeed any horse in all Babylon. But compared to their horse, so my friend said, it was but a lumbering ass that could be beaten with ease.

" 'Then they offered, as a great favor, to permit me to join them in a wager. I was quite carried away with the plan.

" 'Then our horse was badly beaten, and I lost much gold!' Nomasir said, head shaking, while Arkad laughed, but continued, 'Later, I discovered that this was a deceitful plan of those two and they constantly journeyed with caravans seeking victims. Thou see, the person we raced against in Nineveh was their partner and shared among them the bets they won. This shrewd deceit taught me my first lesson in looking out for oneself.

" 'I was soon to learn another, equally bitter lesson. In the caravan was another young person with whom I became quite friendly. Ze was a descendant of wealthy parents in the fur trade. This person found zirself, like me, journeying to Nineveh to find a suitable location to prosper. Not long after our arrival, ze told me of a merchant who had died and whose shop, with its rich merchandise and patronage, could be secured at a paltry price. I was enticed into the deal with this person and that we would be equal partners, but first they must return to Babylon to secure some gold coin. Since time was of the essence, ze prevailed upon me to purchase the stock with my gold, agreeing that their gold would be used later to carry on our venture.

" 'This partner delayed the trip to Babylon for so long, proving in the meantime to be an unwise buyer and a foolish spender. I finally put zir out, but not before the business had deteriorated to where we had only unsalable goods and not enough gold to buy other goods. I sacrificed what was left to an Israelite for a pitiful sum.

" 'Soon there followed, I tell you, my wise parents, bitter days. I sought employment and found it not, for I was without trade or training that would enable me to earn. I sold my horses. I sold my bonded servant. I sold my extra robes so that I might have food and a place to sleep. But each day a small desire began to grow. I had a vision in my dreams of a plow field and a single blooming barley plant. In this dream, the days passed rapidly and this one plant soon spread throughout the whole field.

" 'But in those bitter days, I did remember thy confidence in me, Arkad.

" 'Thou had sent me forth to become a person of good standing, and this, I was determined to accomplish.' Hearing these words from Nomasir, Arkad's spouse buried their face and wept softly. 'At this time, I thought of the tablet that had been given to me upon which thou had carved the five laws of gold. Thereupon, I read most carefully thy words of wisdom, and realized that if I had but sought wisdom first, my gold would not have been lost from my grasp.

" 'I memorized each law by heart and determined that when the time has come and the God of Good Fortune smiled upon me once again, I would be guided by the wisdom of age and not by the inexperience of youth. For the benefit of ye who are seated here this night, I will read the wisdom of Arkad as engraved upon the clay tablet which was given to me ten years ago:

The Five Laws of Gold

I

Gold comes gladly and in increasing quantity to any person who will put by not less than one-tenth of their earnings to create an estate for their future and that of their family.

II

Gold will labor diligently and contentedly for the wise owner who finds for it profitable employment, multiplying it as the flocks in the fields.

III

Gold clings to the protection of the cautious owner who invests it under the advice of people who are wise in gold's handling.

III

I

Gold slips away from the person who invests it in businesses or purposes that they are not familiar with or which are not approved by those skilled in its safe keeping.

III

II

Gold flees from the person who forces it to impossible earnings or follows the alluring advice of tricksters and schemers or trusts it to their own inexperience and romantic desires in investment.

" 'These are the five laws of gold as written by Arkad and gifted to me. I do proclaim them to be of greater value than gold itself, as I will show by the continuance of my tale.'

"Nomasir then again faced Arkad. 'I have told thee of the depth of poverty and despair to which my inexperience brought me. *However, there is no chain of disasters that will not come to an end.* Mine came when I secured employment—managing a crew of bonded servants working upon the new outer wall of the city.

" 'Profiting from my knowledge of the first law of gold, I saved a copper from my first earnings, adding to it at every opportunity until I had a piece of silver. It was a slow procedure, for one must live.

" 'I must admit, I did have to spend grudgingly, because I was determined to earn back the coin that was lost before the 10 years were over.'

"Nomasir continued the tale to a rapt audience. 'One day, the bonded servant master, with whom I had become quite friendly, said to me: 'Thou are a thrifty youth who spends not only of what you earn unlike others. Do thou have gold put by that is not earning?'

" ' 'Yes,' I replied, my curiosity piqued. 'It is my greatest desire to earn gold. For I am determined to replace the ones that were trusted to me by my parents, which I have lost in my journey.'

" ' ' 'Tis a worthy ambition, I will grant,' the master told me, 'and do thou know that the gold which thou have saved can work for thee and earn much more gold?'

" ' 'Alas! My experience has been bitter. The gold Arkad, my wise parent, had so graciously gifted to me has fled and I am in great fear, that my own might do the same in time.'

" 'The master began, 'If thou have confidence in me, I will give thee a lesson in the profitable handling of gold. Within a year the outer wall will be completed and ready for the great gates of bronze that will be built at each entrance to protect the city from the Great Ruler of the City's enemies.'

" 'The master continued with growing excitement, 'In all Nineveh, there is not enough metal to make these gates, and the Great Ruler has not thought to provide for them. Here is my plan: A group of us will pool our gold and send a caravan to the mines of copper and tin, which are distant, and bring the metal for the gates to Nineveh. When the Great Ruler commands, 'Make the great gates,' we alone can supply the metal and shall ask for a rich price. And even if the Great Ruler does not buy from us, we will still possess the metal that can be sold for a fair price.' '

"This offer was unique to Nomasir's previous ventures, so ze said, 'In this offer I recognized an opportunity to abide by the third law and invest my savings under the guidance of wise people. This deal also provided safety, for the metal could be sold for a small profit over time should the Great Ruler not buy. Nor was I disappointed. Our pool was a success, and my small store of gold was greatly increased by the transaction. Luck was upon me and I was prepared for it, as the old saying goes.'

"With a look of subtle pride, Nomasir continued, 'In due time, I was accepted as a member of this same group in our ventures. They were people wise in the profitable handling of gold. They discussed each plan carefully and presented it with great care before entering into an agreement. They would take no risk in losing their principal or tying it up in unprofitable investments from which their gold could not be recovered. Such foolish ventures as the horse race and the partnership I had entered in my inexperience would have scant consideration from them. They would have immediately pointed out the weaknesses in any feeble plan set before them.

" 'Through my association with these people of Nineveh, I learned to safely invest gold to ventures that will bring profitable returns. As the years went on, my treasure increased more and more rapidly. Not only did I make back as much as I lost, but much more.

" 'Through my misfortunes, my trials, and my successes, I have tested time and again the wisdom of the five laws of gold, and Arkad and I have proven them true in every test. For a person who is without knowledge of the five laws, gold comes not often and slips away quickly. But to them who abides by the five laws, gold comes and works as their dutiful bonded servant.'

"Nomasir halted on speaking and motioned a bonded servant in the back of the room. The bonded servant brought forward, one at a time, three heavy leather bags. One of these Nomasir took and placed upon the floor before Arkad's feet, addressing zir again, 'Thou did give to me a bag of gold—Babylon gold. Behold, in its place, I do return to thee a bag of Nineveh gold that is of equal weight. An equal exchange. As will all agree.

" 'Thou did give to me a clay tablet inscribed with wisdom. Behold, in its stead, I do return two bags of gold.' So saying, Nomasir took from the bonded servant the other two bags and, likewise, placed them upon the floor before Arkad.

" 'This is to prove to thee, my wise parent, of how much greater value I consider thy wisdom than thy gold. Yet, who can measure in bags of gold, the value of wisdom? Without it, gold is quickly lost by those who have it. But with wisdom, gold can be secured by those who possess it, as these three bags of gold do prove.

" 'It does, indeed, give to me the deepest satisfaction to stand before thee, my dear parent Arkad, and say that, because of thy wisdom, I have been able to become rich and respected by fellows of good character.'

"Arkad placed a hand fondly upon the head of Nomasir. 'Thou has learned well thy lessons, and I am, indeed, fortunate to have a child to whom I can entrust my wealth.' "

Kalabab ceased the tale and gave a critical look at the listeners. "Friends, what does this tale mean to ye? Who amongst ye can go to thy wise elder and give an account of the excellent handling of their earnings? What would these venerable people think if ye were to say, 'I have traveled much and learned much and labored much and earned much, yet, alas, of gold I have little. Some I spent wisely, some I spent foolishly, and much I lost in reckless ways?' "

Then Kalabab continued to question the listeners, "Do ye still think it as an inconsistency of fate that some people have much gold and others have none to speak of?

"People possess much wealth when they know the five laws of

gold and abide thereby. Because I learned these five laws in my youth and abided by them, I have become a wealthy merchant. Not by some strange magic did I accumulate what I have now.

"Rather, the coin that comes quickly goes the same way. A wealth that stays to offer enjoyment and satisfaction to its owner comes gradually, for it is a child born of knowledge and persistent purpose. Earning wealth is but a slight burden upon the thoughtful person. While bearing its weight consistently from year to year accomplishes the final purpose.

"The five laws of gold offer to ye a rich reward for their observance. Each of these five laws is rich with meaning. Lest ye fail to grasp their depth in the brevity of my tale, I shall now repeat them. I do know them each by heart because in my youth, I saw their value and would not be content until I knew them word for word.

"One. Gold comes gladly and in increasing quantity to any person who will put by not less than one-tenth of their earnings to create an estate for their future and that of their family.

"Any person who will put by one-tenth of their earnings consistently and invest it wisely will definitely create a valuable estate that will provide an income for themselves in the future and further guarantee safety for their family in case the gods call them to the world of darkness. This law always says that gold comes gladly to such a person who can save. I can truly certify this in my own life. The more gold I accumulate, the more readily it comes to me and in increased quantities. The gold which I and ye save earns more, and its earnings earn more, and this is how the first law works on itself.

"Two. Gold will labor diligently and contentedly for the wise owner who finds for its profitable employment, multiplying even as the flocks of the fields.

"Gold, indeed, is a willing worker. It is ever eager to multiply when opportunity presents itself. To every person who has a store of gold set by, opportunity comes for its most profitable use. As the years pass, it multiplies itself in surprising ways.

"Three. Gold clings to the protection of the cautious owner who invests it under the advice of people who are wise in gold's handling.

Gold indeed, clings to the cautious owner, even as it flees the careless owner. The person who seeks the advice of those wise in the handling of gold soon learns not to jeopardize this treasure, but to preserve it in safety and enjoy in contentment its consistent growth and increase.

"Four. Gold slips away from the person who invests it in business or purposes that they are not familiar with or which are not approved by those skilled in its safekeeping.

"To the person who has gold, but is not yet skilled in its handling, many uses may appear highly profitable. Too often, however, these are fraught with the danger of loss, and, if properly analyzed by a wise person, it shows a little possibility of profit. Therefore, the inexperienced owner of gold who trusts in their own judgment and invests it in affairs with which they lack or have no knowledge of too often finds their judgment imperfect, and pays for this inexperience with their wealth. Wise, indeed, is the person who invests their treasures under the guidance of those who are skilled in the ways of gold.

"Five. Gold flees from the person who forces it to impossible earnings or who follows the alluring advice of tricksters and schemers or who trusts it to their own inexperience and romantic desires in investment.

"Fanciful propositions often come to the new owner of gold.

These appear to endow their treasure with magic powers that will enable it to make impossible earnings. Yet heed the wise person, for they know the risks that lurk behind every plan to make great wealth suddenly."

Kalabab continued, "Forget not the rich people of Nineveh who would take no chance of losing their principal or tying it up in unprofitable investments.

"This ends my tale of the five laws of gold. In telling it to ye, I have told the secrets of my own success.

"Yet, these are not secrets, but truths for which every person must first learn and then follow if they wish to step out of the multitude of people that, like wild dogs of the desert sands, must worry each day for food to eat, with no thought of the morrow."

Kalabab motioned towards everyone in the tent. "Tomorrow, we enter Babylon. Look! See the fire that burns eternal above the Temple of Bel! We are already in sight of the golden city. Tomorrow, each of ye shall have gold, the gold each has so well earned by thy faithful services. Ten years from this night, what can ye tell about the gold ye earn on the morrow?

"If there be a person among us, who, like Nomasir, will use a portion of their gold to start for themselves an estate, will they not, henceforth, be wisely guided by the wisdom of Arkad?

"Our wise acts accompany us through life to please and help us. Just as surely, our unwise acts follow us to plague and torment, and alas, they cannot be forgotten. In the front rank of the torments that do follow us are the memories of the things we should have done, of the opportunities which had come to us and we took not.

"Rich are the treasures of Babylon. So rich, no person can count their value in pieces of gold. Each year, these treasures grow richer and more valuable. Like the treasures of every land, they are a reward, a rich reward awaiting those people of purpose who determine their own future. In the strength of thine own desires is a magic power. Guide this power with knowledge of the five laws of gold and ye shall share the treasures of Babylon."

BETTER A LITTLE CAUTION THAN A GREAT REGRET

Parable 13

FIFTY-FIVE PIECES of gold! Never before had Rodan, the spear maker of old Babylon, carried so much gold in a leather wallet tied to a waistband strap beneath zir robe. Happily, down the Great Ruler of the City's Smith Street Rodan strode. Cheerfully, the gold clinked as the wallet, belted to the hip, swayed with each step. It was the sweetest music humble Rodan had ever heard.

Fifty-five pieces of gold! All to their own. Rodan could hardly realize the good fortune. What power was in those clinking discs! Ze could purchase anything a person wanted. A grand house, land, cattle, camels, horses, chariots... whatever might be a desire.

What use should Rodan make of it? That evening, as ze turned into a side street toward the home of a sibling, Rodan could think of nothing ze would rather possess than those same glittering, heavy pieces of gold. It was upon another evening some days later that a perplexed Rodan entered the shop of Mathon, the lender of gold and the dealer in jewels and rare fabrics. Glancing neither to the right nor left of the colorful articles artfully displayed, Rodan passed through to the living quarters at the rear. Here, the spear maker found the lender lounging upon a rug and partaking of a meal served by a bonded servant.

Mathon, the Lender of Gold

"I desire to consult with thee for I know not what to do," Rodan said, standing stolidly with feet apart, hairy chest exposed by the gaping front of a leather jacket.

Mathon's narrow, sallow face smiled a friendly greeting. "What indiscretions have thou done so that thou should seek the lender of gold? Have thou been unlucky at the gaming tables? Or hath some plump dame entangled thee? For many years I have known thee, yet never have thou sought me to aid thee in thy troubles."

"No, no. Not such as that. I seek no gold. Instead, I crave thy wise advice."

"Hear! Hear! What does this person say? No one comes to the lender of gold for advice. My ears must play me false."

"They listen true," Rodan replied with a slight smile on zir lips.

"Can this be so? Rodan, the spear maker, did display more cunning than all the rest, for this spear maker came to Mathon, not for gold, but for advice. Many people come to me for gold to pay for their follies, but advice they do not seek. Yet who is more able to advise on matters of gold than the lender of gold?"

"Thou shall eat with me, Rodan," Mathon continued. "Thou shall be my guest for the evening." Looking to the bonded servant, Mathon said, "Rodan, the spear maker, who comes for advice, shall be my honored guest. Bring much food and get the largest cup."

Mathon turned to Rodan again and said, "Now, tell me what troubles thee."

"It is the gift bestowed upon me by the Great Ruler of the City."

Mathon looked perplexed. "The Great Ruler's gift? The Great Ruler of our great city gave thou a gift and it is giving thee troubles? What manner of gift is this?"

"Because the ruler was much pleased with the design I did submit for a new point on the spears of the Royal Guard, the Great Ruler of the City did present me with fifty pieces of gold. And now I am much perplexed." Rodan looked down at zir hands. "I am beseeched, each hour the sun travels across the sky, by those who would seek me to share it with them."

"That is natural. More people want gold that can be acquired quickly and would wish for one who comes by it easily to divide it. But can thou not say 'No?' Is thy will not as strong as thy mighty arms?"

Rodan looked away. "To many, I can say 'No.' Yet sometimes, it would be easier to say 'Yes.' Can one refuse to share a blessing with one's sibling to whom they are deeply devoted?"

Mathon looked mischievously back. "Surely, thy own sibling would not wish to deprive thee of enjoyment of thy award?"

"But it is for the sake of Araman—my sibling's life partner, to whom they wish to succeed as a rich merchant. My sibling does feel that Araman has never had a chance, and beseeches me to loan this gold so that ze may become a prosperous merchant and repay me from the future profits."

"My friend," resumed Mathon, " 'Tis a worthy subject thou brought to discuss. Gold brings unto its holder responsibility and a changed position with your social companions. It also brings fear lest it is lost or taken by tricks. The tricks being subtle or obvious. Gold brings a feeling of power and ability to do good. Conversely, it brings opportunities whereby old friends with very good intentions may bring difficulties upon thyself.

"Did thou ever hear of the farmer of Nineveh who could understand the language of animals? I suspect not. 'Tis not the kind of tale to likely be told over a bronze caster's forge. I will tell it to thee, for thou should know that borrowing and lending has more to it than just the mere passing of gold from the hands of one to the hands of another.

"This farmer, who could understand what the animals said to each other, lingered in the farmyard each evening just to listen to their words. One night the farmer did hear the ox bemoaning to the ass of the hardness of an ox's lot:

" 'I do labor pulling the plow from morning until night. No matter how hot the day is, or how tired my legs are, or how the bow does chafe my neck. I still must work. But you are a creature of leisure. You are bestowed with a colorful blanket and do nothing more than carry our master wherever ze wishes to go. When the master goes nowhere you do rest and eat the green grass all day.'

"Now, the ass, a goodly fellow, sympathized with the ox and said:

" 'My good friend, you do work very hard, and I would help ease your lot. Therefore, will I tell you how you may have a day of rest. In the morning, when the bonded servant comes to fetch you to the plow, lie upon the ground and bellow much that the bonded servant must think you are sick and cannot work.'

"So, the ox took the advice of the ass and the next morning the bonded servant returned to the farmer and said the ox was sick and cannot work.

" 'Then,' said the farmer, 'hitch the ass to the plows for the plowing must go on.'

"That whole day, the ass, who had only intended to help a friend, found themself compelled to do the ox's task. When the night came, the ass was released from the plow with a bitter heart, weary legs and a sore neck—where the box had chafed it all day long.

"The farmer lingered in the barnyard to listen once more. The ox spoke first. 'You are my good friend. Because of your wise advice, I have enjoyed a day of rest.'

" 'And I,' retorted the ass, 'am like many other simple-hearted ones who start helping a friend and end up doing their work for them instead. Hereafter, you must draw your own plow, for I did hear the master command the bonded servant to send for the butcher if you were still sick on the morrow... I wish though that the farmer would send for the butcher, for you are a lazy being.'

"Thereafter, they spoke to each other no more and ended their friendship. Can thou tell me the moral of this tale?" asked Mathon.

" 'Tis a good tale," responded Rodan, "but I see not the moral."

"I thought not that you would. But it is there and simple too. Just this: *if thou desire to help thy friends, do so in a way that will not bring thy friends burdens upon thyself.*"

"I had not thought of that. It is a wise moral indeed. I wish not to assume the burdens of my sibling's life partner. But tell me, thou lend out too many, do not the borrowers repay?"

Mathon smiled—the smile of a person whose soul is rich with much experience.

"Can a loan be well made if the borrower cannot repay?" the lender asked. "Must not the lender be wise and judge carefully whether their gold can serve a useful purpose to the borrower so it can be returned to the lender once more? Or will the loan be wasted by the borrower unable to use it wisely, thus losing the lender's treasure and burdening the borrower with a debt that cannot be paid? I will show thee the tokens in my token chest and let them tell their own stories."

Into the room, Mathon brought a chest as long as an arm. It was covered with red pigskin and ornamented with bronze designs. Mathon placed it upon the floor and squatted before it, both hands resting upon the lid.

"From each person to whom I lend," Mathon continued, "I do extract a token for my token chest, to remain there until the loan is repaid. When they repay, I give back the token. If they never repay, it will always remind me of one who was not faithful to my confidence.

"The safest loans, my token box tells me, are for those whose possessions are of more value than the one they desire. They own lands, jewels, camels, or other things which can be sold to repay the loan. Some of the tokens given to me are jewels of more value than the loan. Others are promises that, if the loan is not repaid as agreed, they will deliver to me certain property settlements. On loans like those I am assured that my gold will be returned with the rental thereon, for the loan is based on property.

"In another class, there are those who have the capacity to earn. They are such as thou, who labor or serve and are paid. They have income and if they are honest and suffer no misfortune, I know that they too can also repay the gold I have lent them and the rental to which I am entitled. Such loans are based on human effort.

"Still, others are those who have neither property nor assured earning capacity. Life is hard, and there will always be some who cannot adjust themselves to it. Alas, for the loans I give them, even though they are no larger than a pence, my token box may censure me in the years to come unless they be guaranteed by good friends of the borrower who know them to be of honor."

Mathon released the clasp of the chest and opened the lid. Rodan leaned forward eagerly. At the top of the chest, a bronze neck piece lay upon a scarlet cloth. Mathon picked up the piece and patted it affectionately.

"This shall always remain in my token chest," Mathon said, "for the owner has passed on into the Land of the Darkness. I treasure it, their token, and I treasure their memory. For they were my good friend. We traded together with much success until my friend brought a significant other to wed, one who came from the East. A beautiful and dazzling creature this spouse-to-be was. It caused my friend to spend great amounts of gold in order to gratify their lover's desires.

"My friend came to me one morning in great distress when their gold was gone. I counseled with them and offered a hand, saying that I would help them once more become the master of their own affairs. My friend swore by the sign of the Great Bull that this would be so, but it was not to be. In a quarrel, the spouse thrust a knife into the heart of my friend."

"And what has become of the spouse?" questioned Rodan.

"Yes, of course, this was theirs," Mathon responded, picking up just the scarlet cloth. "In bitter remorse, the spouse jumped into the Euphrates, never to be heard of again. These two loans will never be repaid. The chest tells you, Rodan, that humans in the throes of great emotions are not safe risks for the gold lender."

After spending a somber mood for but a few heartbeats, Mathon reached once more into the chest for a ring carved of ox bone.

"Here! Now this is different. This belongs to a farmer, Daon, from whom I bought rugs. The locusts came once and they had no food to eat besides Daon's crops, which left this farmer destitute. I helped Daon for the next season and when the new crop came in, Daon repaid me. Later, Daon came again and told of strange goats in a distant land as described by a traveler. They had long hair so fine and soft it would weave into rugs more beautiful than any ever seen in Babylon. Daon wanted a herd but had not the coin. So, I did lend zir the gold to make the journey and bring back the goats. Now Daon's herd has begun, and next year, I shall surprise the lords of Babylon with the most expensive rugs that have been their good fortune to buy. Soon I must return the ring. Daon does insist on repaying promptly."

"Some borrowers do that?" questioned Rodan.

"If they borrow gold for meaningful purposes, then that will bring money back to them—I find it good. But if they borrow because of their indiscretions, I find this not to be so. I loan to thee with great caution so that I may have my hard-earned gold back in hand again."

"Tell me about this one," requested Rodan, picking up a heavy gold bracelet inset with jewels in rare designs.

"Ah, shiny it is, and it does appeal to my good friend," bantered Mathon.

"I am still much younger than thou," retorted Rodan.

"I grant that. The owner of this is Mari, who is fat and wrinkled and does talk so much yet says so little that this person drives me mad. Once, they had much money and were good customers, but ill times came upon them. Mari had ambitions of zir child becoming a great merchant. Mari came to me and borrowed gold so that the child may become a partner of a caravan owner who travels on camels to barter in one city what was bought in another.

"This trader, who Mari's offspring went into business with, proved to be a rascal, for they left the child of Mari in a distant city without money and without friends, departing early while the youth slept. Perhaps, when this youth has grown to personhood, they will repay. Until then, I received no rental for the loan, only much talk. But I do admit, the jewels are worthy of the loan."

"Did Mari ask thy advice as to the wisdom of the loan?" asked Rodan.

Mathon gave a weak smile. "Quite otherwise. Mari had pictured zirself as the parent of a wealthy and powerful citizen of Babylon. To suggest otherwise was to infuriate Mari. A fair rebuke I had received. I knew the risk for this inexperienced child, but as ze offered security for the loan, I could not refuse."

"This," continued Mathon, waving a bit of pack rope tied into a knot, "belongs to Nebatur, the camel trader. When they would buy a herd larger than their funds allow for, Nebatur brings to me this knot, and I then lend according to their needs. This camel trader is a wise one. I have confidence in their good judgment and can lend to Nebatur freely. Many other merchants of Babylon have my confidence because of their honorable behavior. Their tokens come and go frequently in my token box. Good merchants are an asset to our city, and it benefits me to aid them and keep the trade moving so that Babylon may continue to be prosperous."

Mathon picked out a beetle carved in turquoise and tossed it contemptuously on the floor. "A bug from Egypt. The fellow who owns this does not care whether I ever receive my gold back. Whenever I approach zir, the reply is always, 'How can I repay when ill fate pursues me? Thou have plenty more,' What can I do? The token is of their parent—a worthy farmer of small means who pledged their land and herd to back the foolish enterprises of youth. The youth found success at first but then were overzealous to gain great wealth.

"Their knowledge was immature, and their enterprises collapsed. Youth is ambitious and would take quicker paths to wealth and the desirable things for which it stands. To secure wealth quickly, youth often borrow unwisely. Alas, it is not entirely their fault. For the youth, who never had enough experience in handling wealth, was too naive to realize that hopeless debt is like a deep abyss into which one may descend quickly and where one may struggle vainly for many seasons. It is a pit of sorrow and regret where the brightness of the sun is overcast, and nights are made unhappy by restless sleep.

"Yet, I do not discourage the borrowing of gold; I encourage it. I recommend it if it is for a wise purpose. I myself made my first real success as a merchant with borrowed gold," Mathon looked down at zir hands, "Yet, what should the lender do in such a case? The youth is in despair and accomplishes nothing. They are discouraged and makes no effort to repay. My heart is torn against depriving the parent of their land and cattle."

"Thou tell me much of which I am interested in hearing," ventured Rodan, "but I hear no answer to my question. Should I lend my fifty pieces of gold to my sibling's significant other? They mean much to me."

"Well, thy sibling is a sterling person whom I do much esteem. Should thy sibling's significant other come to me and ask to borrow fifty pieces of gold, I should ask them for what purpose it will be used. If the significant other answers that they desire to become a merchant like me and deal with jewels and rich furnishings, I would say, 'What knowledge do thou have of the ways of trade? Do thou know where thou can buy at the lowest of costs? Do thou know where to sell at a fair price?' Can this person say 'yes' to these questions, Rodan?"

"No, they cannot," Rodan admitted. "This person has helped me much in making spears and has assisted some in the shops, though."

"Then I will say to them that this pursuit is not wise. Merchants must learn their trade. This ambition, though worthy, is not practical, and I will not lend to them any gold." Mathon continued, "But, supposing a person can say, 'Yes, I have helped merchants much. I know how to travel to Smyrna and buy at low cost the rugs that are made in the homes of the workers. I also know many of the rich people of Babylon to whom I can sell these at a large profit,' then I will say, 'Your purpose is wise and your ambition is honorable. I shall be glad to lend to thee the fifty pieces of gold if thou can give me security that they will be returned.'

"But if a person says, 'I have no security other than that I am an honored person and will pay thee well for the loan,' then I will reply, 'I treasure much each piece of gold. Were the robbers to take it from thee as thou journeyed to Smyrna or snatch the rugs from thee as thou returned, then thou would have no means of repaying me, and my gold would be gone.'

"Gold, thou see, Rodan, is the merchandise of the lender of money. It is easy to lend. If it is lent unwisely, then it is difficult to get back. The wise lender wishes not the risk of the undertaking but the guarantee of safe repayment. 'Tis well to assist those who are in trouble, 'tis well to help those upon whom fate has laid a heavy hand. 'Tis well to help those who are starting, so that they may progress and become valuable citizens. But help must be given wisely, lest, like the farmer's ass, in our desire to help we take

upon ourselves the burden that belongs to another.

“Again, I wandered from thy question, Rodan, but hear my answer: Keep thy fifty pieces of gold. What thy labor earns for thee and what is given to thee are thy rewards, and no person can put an obligation upon thee to part with such rewards unless it be thy wish. If thou will lend that gold so that it, too, may begin to earn for thee even more, then lend with caution and in many places. I do not like idle gold, but I like risk even less. Tell me, how many years has thou labored as a spear maker?”

“Fully three.”

“How much besides this great gift has thou saved?”

“Three gold pieces.”

“To wit, for each year that thou has labored and denied thyself good things in life, thou has saved from thy earnings just one gold coin?”

“Yes, it is as thou say.”

“Then, can it be said that in fifty years of labor, thou can accumulate fifty pieces of gold by thy self-practicing self-denial?”

“Yes, a lifetime of labor it would be.”

“Do thou think thy sibling would wish to jeopardize the savings of fifty years of labor over the bronze melting pot so that their spouse might experiment on being a merchant?”

“Not if I speak thy words.”

“Then, go to thy sibling and say, ‘Three years I have labored each day, from morning until night, except for the fast days. I have denied myself many things that my heart has craved. For each year of labor and self-denial I have to show one piece of gold. Thou are my favored sibling, and I wish that thy significant other may engage in a business in which they would prosper greatly. If they will submit to me a plan that seems wise and possible to my friend, Mathon, then I will gladly lend to them my savings of an entire year so that they may have an opportunity to prove that they can succeed.' Do that, I say, and if they have it within themselves to succeed, then they can prove it. If they fail, they will not owe thee more than what may someday be repaid through their usual labors.

"I am a gold lender because I possess more gold than I can use in my own trade. I desire my surplus of gold to labor for others and thereby earn more gold. I do not wish to take the risk of losing my gold for I have labored much and denied myself much to secure it. Therefore, I will no longer lend any of it to ventures where I am not confident that it is safe and will be returned to me. Neither will I lend it to ones where I am not convinced that their earnings will be promptly paid to me.

"I have told thee, Rodan, a few secrets of my token chest. From them, thou may understand the weakness of people and their eagerness to borrow that which they have no certain means to repay. From this, thou can see how often their high hopes of the great earnings they could make, if they but had gold, are but false hopes that they have not the ability or training to fulfill.

"Thou, Rodan, now has gold which thou should put to earning more gold for thee. Thou are about to become even as I am, a gold lender. If thou do safely preserve your treasure, it will produce liberal earnings for thee and be a rich source of pleasure and profit during all thy days. But if thou do let it escape like sand through fingers, it will be a source of constant sorrow and regret for as long as thy memory does last." Looking Rodan straight in the eye, Mathon asked, "What is thy greatest desire for this gold in thy wallet?"

"To keep it safe."

"Wisely spoken," replied Mathon approvingly. "Thy first desire is for safety. Do you think that, in the custody of thy sibling, it would be truly safe from possible loss?"

"I fear not, for neither of them is wise in guarding gold."

"*Then be not swayed by foolish sentiments of obligation to trust thy treasure to any person*. If thou would help thy family or friends, find other ways that would not risk the loss of thy own treasure. Forget not that gold slips away in unexpected ways, especially from those who are unskilled in guarding it," lectured Mathon, "as well waste thy treasure in extravagance as to let others lose it for thee. So, Rodan, after ensuring its safety, what do thou desire with your treasure?"

"That it earns more gold."

With a wan smile, Mathon replied, "Again, thou speak with wisdom. Gold should be made to earn and grow larger. Gold wisely lent may even double itself with its earnings before a person like thyself grows old. But if thou risk losing it, thou also risk losing all that might have earned.

"Therefore, be not swayed by the fantastic plans of impractical people who think they see ways to force thy gold to make earnings unusually large. Such plans are the creations of dreamers who are unskilled in the safe and dependable laws of trade. Be conservative in what thou expect it to earn so that thou may keep and enjoy this hard-earned treasure. *To put it to work with a promise of fantastic returns is to invite loss*. So, seek to associate thyself with people and enterprises whose success is established so that thy treasure may earn liberally under their skillful use and be guarded safely by their wisdom and experience.

"Thus, may thou avoid the misfortunes that follow most of the children of people whom the gods see fit to entrust with gold."

When Rodan tried to thank zir for the wise advice, Mathon would not listen, cutting off Rodan, saying, "The Great Ruler of the City's gift shall teach thee much wisdom. If thou wish to keep thy fifty pieces of gold, thou must be discreet indeed. Many uses will tempt thee. Much advice will be spoken to thee. Numerous opportunities to make large profits will be offered to thee. The stories from my token box should warn thee, before thou let any piece of gold leave thy pouch, be sure that thou have a safe way to pull it back again. Should my further advice appeal to thee, return again, as it will gladly be given.

"Now, Rodan, come here and look at this inscription on the lid of the box. If thou can read, say it out loud..."

Better a little caution, than a great regret.

ADVICE FROM AN OLD SOLDIER

Parable 14

THERE ZE STOOD, old Banzar, a grim warrior of another day, standing guard at the passageway leading to the top of the ancient walls of Babylon. Above, valiant defenders were battling to hold the walls. Upon them depended the future existence of this great city with its many thousands of citizens.

Over the walls came the roar of the attacking armies, the yelling of countless soldiers, the trampling of thousands of horses, and the deafening boom of the battering rams pounding against the bronze gates.

In the street behind the gate lounged the old spearperson, Banzar, ready to defend the entrance should the gates give way. There were but a precious few for the task; the main armies of Babylon were with the Great Ruler of the City, far away in the East, on the great expedition against the Elamites. With the armies gone and no attack upon the city having been anticipated, the defending forces were thus small.

Unexpectedly, from the north, the mighty Assyrian armies bore down. Now the walls must hold, or Babylon was doomed.

Around Banzar gathered great crowds of citizens, pale-faced and terrified, eagerly seeking news of the battle. With hushed awe, they watched the stream of wounded and dead being carried or led out of the passageway, where the crucial point of attack was. After three days of circling the great city, the enemy had suddenly thrown their great strength against this section and this one gate.

The defenders on the top of the wall fought off the attackers' scaffold platforms and the scaling ladders using arrows, burning oil, and, if any reached the top, spears. Against the defenders, thousands of the enemy's archers poured a deadly barrage of arrows.

Old Banzar had the best vantage point for the news. For ze was closest to the conflict and the first to hear each fresh repulse of the frenzied attackers.

An elderly merchant crowded close to the old spearperson. With quivering hands, the merchant spoke, "Tell me! Tell me! They cannot get in. My children march with the Great Ruler of the City's armies. There is no one to protect my lover, who is as old as I am," The merchant took a breath and continued, "My goods, they will steal them all. My food, they will leave nothing. We are old, too old to defend ourselves–too old to be pressed into bonded servantry. We shall starve. We shall die. Tell me they cannot get in!"

"Calm thyself, good merchant," the spearperson responded. "The walls of Babylon are strong. Go back to the bazaar and tell thy spouse that the walls will protect ye and all thy possessions as safely as they protect the rich treasures of our Great Ruler of the City. Keep close to the walls and mind the shade, lest the arrows flying over strike thee!"

***

As the old merchant withdrew, a person with a baby in their arms took their place. "Sergeant," the person said, "what news from the top? Tell me truly so that I may reassure my poor spouse. Ze lies with fever from a terrible arrow in the leg yet insist upon donning zir armor and spear to protect me, because I am with a child. Terrible, my spouse says, will be the vengeful lust of our enemies should they break in."

"Be of good heart," Banzar said. "The walls of Babylon will protect thee and thy babies. They are high and strong. Hear thee the battle cries of our valiant defenders as they empty the caldrons of burning oil upon the ladder climbers!"

"Yes, that I do hear, but also the roar of the battering rams hammering at our very gates."

"Return to thy lover. Tell them the gates are strong and will withstand the rams. Also, the climbers of the ladders upon the outer walls have nothing awaiting them in our city besides a swift spear thrust. Watch thy way home and mind the shadows for as thou know, arrows abound today."

The spearperson stepped aside to clear the passage for heavily armed reinforcements. As, with clanking bronze shields and heavy treads, they tramped by, a small citizen plucked at the spearperson's tunic.

"Tell me, please, soldier, are we safe?" The child pleaded. "I hear the awful noises. I see the soldiers all bleeding. I am so frightened! What will become of our family, of my parents or my two little siblings?"

The grim old campaigner blinked, thrust forward zir chin, and beheld the child. "Be not afraid, little one. The walls of Babylon will protect thee and thy parents and siblings. These mighty walls the old Great Ruler Semiramis built over a hundred years ago are for the safety of people such as you. Never have they been broken through. Go back and tell thy parent and siblings that Babylon will protect them, and they need have no fear."

***

Day after day, the spearperson, an old hand at soldiering, stood at their post, watching as reinforcements piled into the passageway, ready to fight until they returned—wounded or dead. Around them, frightened citizens gathered endlessly, eager to know if the walls would hold.

To all who asked, the spearperson gave the answer with the fine dignity of an old soldier, "The walls of Babylon will protect ye."

For three weeks and five days the attack waged with scarcely ceasing violence. The old spearperson's jaw grew harder and grimmer as the passage behind, wet with the blood of countless wounded, was churned into mud by the relentless streams of soldiers passing up and staggering back down. Each day, attackers were slaughtered and their bodies piled in heaps before the walls. Each night, their comrades carried them back to be buried.

After the fifth night of the fourth week of this clamor without diminish, the first streaks of daylight, illuminating the plains, disclosed great clouds of dust raised by the retreating armies.

A mighty shout went up from the defenders. There was no mistaking its meaning. The waiting troops behind the walls resounded the cry, which was echoed by the citizens upon the streets. It swept over the city with the violence of a storm.

People rushed from their houses. The throbbing mob jammed the streets. The pent-up fear of weeks found an outlet in the wild chorus of joy. From the top of the high tower of the Temple of Bel burst forth the flames of victory. Skyward floated the column of blue smoke to carry the message far and wide.

The walls of Babylon had once again repulsed a mighty and vicious foe determined to loot their rich treasures and to ravish and enslave its honorable citizens. *Babylon endured, century after century, because it was fully protected. It could not afford to be otherwise.*

The walls of Babylon were an outstanding example of a person's need and desire for protection.

This desire, inherent within the human race, would be just as strong in the future as it was in ancient Babylon, but people would develop broader and better plans to accomplish the same purpose.

In that future, behind the impregnable walls of insurance, savings accounts, and dependable investments, people could guard themselves against the unexpected tragedies that might enter any door and seat before any fireside.

People could not afford to be without adequate protection.

THE CAMEL TRADER OF BABYLON

Parable 15

THE HUNGRIER ONE BECAME, the clearer one's mind worked. Also, the more sensitive one would become to the odors of food.

Tarkad, the offspring of Azure, certainly thought so. For two whole days, Tarkad had tasted no food except two small figs purloined from over the wall of a garden and had not managed to grab another before the angry gardener rushed forth and chased zir down the street. The shrill cries of that person were still ringing within zir ears as Tarkad walked through the marketplace.

Never before had Tarkad realized how much food was brought to the markets of Babylon and how good it smelled. Leaving the market, Tarkad walked toward the inn and paced back and forth in front of the eating house. Perhaps here, there might be someone familiar.

In distraction, Tarkad unexpectedly found zirself face-to-face with the one person ze wished the most to avoid—the tall bony figure of Dabasir, the camel trader. Of all the friends and others from whom ze had borrowed small sums from, Dabasir made Tarkad feel the most uncomfortable because of the failure to keep a promise to repay promptly.

Dabasir's face beamed at the sight of Tarkad, "Ha! 'Tis Tarkad, just the one I have been seeking so that I might be repaid the two pieces of copper which I lent out a moon ago. Also, the piece of silver which I lent before that. We are well met! I can make good use of the coins this very day. What say you? Hmm?"

Tarkad's face flushed and ze stuttered. Tarkad had an empty stomach, and if any coins were in their pocket, they surely would have gone to nourishment already. "I am sorry, so very sorry," came the mumbled reply, "but today I have neither the copper nor the silver with which I can repay."

"Then get it," Dabasir insisted. "Surely you can get hold of a few coppers and a piece of silver to repay the generosity of an old friend of your parent who aided you when you were in need."

Looking at zir feet, Tarkad said, "It is because ill fortune does follow me that I cannot repay."

"Ill fortune? Would you blame the gods for your own weakness? Ill fortune follows every person who thinks more of borrowing than of repaying. Come with me, youth, while I eat. I am hungry and will tell you a tale."

Tarkad flinched from the brutal frankness of Dabasir, but here at last was an invitation to enter the coveted doorway of the eating house.

Dabasir spoke with a person at the door, and the pair was led into a far corner of the room where they seated themselves upon small rugs.

When Kushor, the proprietor, appeared smiling, Dabasir addressed zir with a slight smile and the usual freedom Dabasir was so fond of, "You look like a fat lizard of the desert! Bring me a goat leg, browned with much juice and bread, and all of the vegetables, for I am hungry and want much food. And do not forget my friend here. Bring them a jug of water. Have it cooled, for the day is hot."

Tarkad's heart sank, and thought, must one sit here and only drink water while watching this creditor devour an entire goat leg? Tarkad said nothing. For nothing could be thought of to say.

Dabasir, however, knew no such thing as silence. Smiling and waving a hand good-naturedly to the other customers, all of whom knew Dabasir, ze said, "I did hear from a traveler just returned from Urfa of a certain rich person with a piece of stone cut so thin one can look through it. They put it in the window of their house to keep out the rain. It is yellow, so relates to this traveler, and upon looking through it, one could see the outside world appear strange. It looks not like what it really is. What say you to that, Tarkad? Do you think all the world could look a different color to a person than what it is?"

"I dare say," responded the youth, much more interested in the fat goat leg placed before Dabasir.

"Well, I know it to be true, for I myself have seen the world in a different color from what it really is, and the tale I am about to tell relates to how I came to see this world in its right and proper color once more."

***

"Dabasir will tell a tale," whispered a neighboring diner to their guest, dragging their rugs a bit closer. Other diners brought their food and crowded into a semi-circle. Sounds of mastication crunched noisily in Tarkad's ears and meaty bones brushed zir arms. Tarkad alone was without food, but Dabasir neither offered to share nor even motioned zir to a small corner of the hard bread that broke off and fell to the floor.

"The tale I am about to tell," began Dabasir, pausing to bite a goodly chunk of the goat leg, "relates to my early life and how I came to be a camel trader. Did anyone know that I once was a bonded servant in Syria?"

A murmur of surprise ran through the audience to which

Dabasir listened with satisfaction.

"When I was young," Dabasir continued, "I learned the trade of my parent, the making of saddles. I worked with my parent in their shop and later took for myself a spouse.

"Being young and not greatly skilled, I earned but little, just enough to support my excellent partner in a modest way. I craved the good things in life for which I could not afford. Soon I found the shopkeepers would trust me to pay later even though I could not settle it immediately.

"Being young and inexperienced, I did not know that the person who spends more than they earn is sowing the seeds of needless self-indulgence, from which they are sure to reap the whirlwinds of luxuries but beyond their means, as did I for my good partner and our home. I paid as I could and for a while, all went well. But in time, I discovered I could not use my earnings both to live upon and pay my debts.

"Creditors began to pursue me to pay for my extravagant purchases and my life became miserable. I borrowed from my friends but could not repay them either. Does this sound familiar, Tarkad? Things went from bad to worse. My good spouse returned to their parents. Thus, alone and surrounded by misery, I decided to leave Babylon and seek another city where young people might have better chances.

"For two years I had a restless, unsuccessful life working for caravan traders. For this I fell in with a set of likeable robbers who scoured the desert for unarmed caravans. Such deeds were unworthy of the offspring of my parents, but I was seeing the world through a colored stone and did not realize to what degradation I had fallen.

"We met with success on our first trip, capturing a rich haul of gold and silks and other valuable wears. This loot we took to Ginir and squandered it all. The second time we were not so fortunate. Just after we had made our capture, we were attacked by the spear-wielding warriors of a native chief who paid for the caravan's protection. Our two leaders were killed, and the rest of us were taken to Damascus where we were stripped of our clothing and sold as bonded servants."

By this point in the story, the whole room was wrapped in a divine silence.

Dabasir continued, "I was purchased for two pieces of silver by a Syrian desert chief. With my hair sheared low and a loin cloth to wrap around my personhood, I was not so different from the other bonded servants. Being a reckless youth, I thought it merely an adventure until my master took me before their four spouses and told them they could have me as their servant—after I was neutered.

"Then, indeed, at that moment I came to realize the hopelessness of my situation. These peoples of the desert were fierce and warlike. I was subject to their will without weapons or means of escape.

"Fearful I stood, as those four spouses looked over me. I wondered if I could expect pity from them. Sira, the first spouse, was different from the others. Zir face was impassive as ze looked upon me. I turned from Sira with little consultation. The next was a contemptuous beauty who gazed at me indifferently as if I had been a mere worm of the earth. The two younger ones tittered as though this was all an exciting joke.

"It seemed like an age that I stood awaiting my sentence. Each of them appeared willing to let the others decide. Finally, Sira spoke up in a cold voice, 'Of neutered servants we have plenty. But of camel tenders we have few, and those few are a worthless lot. Even on this day, I would visit my dear parent, sick with fever, and there is no bonded servant I would trust to lead my camel.

Ask this slave if they can lead a camel.'

"My master thereupon questioned me, 'What know thee of camels?' Striving to conceal my eagerness, I replied, 'I can make them kneel. I can load them. I can lead them on long journeys without being tired. If need be, I can repair their trappings.'

" 'The bonded servant speaks forward enough,' observed my master. 'If thou so desires, Sira, take this one for thy camel tender.'

"So, I was turned over to Sira. That very day, I did lead their camel upon a long journey to Sira's sick parent. I took the occasion to thank them for their intercession and also to tell them that I was not a bonded servant by birth, but the child of a free person, an honorable saddle maker of Babylon. I also told Sira much of my story. Their comments were disconcerting to me, and I pondered much afterwards on what was said.

"Sira began, 'How can you call yourself a free person when your weakness has brought you to this? If a person has within thyself the soul of a bonded servant, will they not become one regardless of birth? Like how water poured into a bowl seeks its level. If a person has within themselves the soul of a free person, will they not become respected and honored in their own city in spite of this misfortune?' "

***

"For over a year I was a bonded servant dwelling among my kind, yet I could not become one of them. One day, Sira asked me, 'In the evening, when the other bonded servants can mingle and enjoy each other's society, why do you sit in the tent alone?'

"I then replied, 'I am pondering what you have told me. I wonder if I do have the soul of a bonded servant. I cannot join them, so I must sit apart.'

" 'I, too, must sit apart,' Sira confided. 'My dowry was large, and my lord married me because of it. Yet they do not desire me. What every person longs for is to be desired. Because of this and because I am barren and have not produced any offspring, I must sit apart. Were I a person like you, I would rather die than be a bonded servant. But the convention of our tribe, somewhat, makes bonded servants of us spouses too.'

" 'What do you think of me by this time?' I asked Sira suddenly. 'Have I the soul of a bonded servant or that of a free person?'

" 'Do you have a desire to repay the just debts you owe in Babylon?' Sira parried.

" 'Yes,' I said, 'I have the desire. But I see no way to do this.'

"Sira then resumed, 'If you contentedly let the years slip by and make no effort to repay, then you have but the contemptible soul of a bonded servant. No person is otherwise who cannot respect themselves and no person can respect themselves who does not repay honest debts.'

" 'But what can I do? I'm a Syrian bonded servant.'

"With a thorny voice, Sira retorted, 'Stay a bonded servant in Syria, you weakling.'

" 'I am not a weakling,' I denied hotly.

" 'Then prove it,' ze said.

" 'How?'

"Sira answered with a question, 'Does the Great Ruler of Babylon fight the enemies in every way ze can and with every force ze has?'

"After a pause, Sira continued, 'Your debts are your enemies.

They ran you out of Babylon. Then you left them alone, but they grew too strong for you. Had you fought them as an honorable person, you could have conquered them and been the one honored among the townspeople. But you had not the soul to fight them, and thus, your pride has gone down until you became a bonded servant of Syria.'

"Much I have thought over Sira's unkind accusations and many defensive phrases I worded to prove myself not a bonded servant at heart, but I was not to have the chance to use them. Three days later, a steward of Sira took me into Sira's tent.

" 'My parent is again very sick,' Sira said. 'Saddle the two best camels in the tribe leader's herd. Tie on water skins and saddlebags for a long journey. The steward will give you food at the kitchen tent.' I packed the camels wondering much at the hefty quantity of provisions the steward provided, for it was less than a day's journey. The steward rode the rear camel which followed, and I led the camel of Sira. It just got dark when we reached the destination. Sira dismissed the steward and said to me, 'Dabasir, have you the soul of a free person or that of a bonded servant?'

" 'The soul of a free person,' I insisted.

" 'Then now is thy chance to prove it. Your master has drunk deeply, and the chiefs are in a stupor. Take these camels and make your escape. Here in this bag is your master's raiment to disguise yourself. I will say you stole the camels and ran away while I visited my sick parent.'

" 'You have the soul of a god,' I told Sira. 'Much I wish that I might lead you to happiness.'

" 'Happiness,' Sira responded, 'does not await the runaway spouse who seeks it in far lands among strange people. Go your own way and may the Gods of the Desert protect you, for the journey is far and barren of food or water.'

"I needed no further urging. I thanked Sira warmly and set away into the night. I was not familiar with this strange country and had only a dim idea of the direction in which lay Babylon. Still, I struck out bravely across the desert toward the hills. One camel I rode while the other I led. All that night and the next day, I traveled, urged on by the knowledge of the terrible fate that was given to bonded servants who stole their master's property and escaped.

"Evening turned to morning and soon came the late afternoon. I reached a rough country as uninhabitable as the desert. The sharp rocks bruised the feet of my faithful camels, forcing them to pick their way slowly and painfully. I met neither person nor beast and could well understand why they shunned this inhospitable land. Never before have I left the routes of the caravans, and now I know why.

"It was such a journey across the wastelands that few people could live and tell a similar story. Day after day, my last camel and I plodded along. Food and water gave out. The heat of the sun was merciless. At the end of the ninth day, I slid from the back of my camel with the feeling that I was too weak to ever remount, and I would surely die, lost in this abandoned country.

"I stretched out upon the ground and slept, not waking until the first gleam of daylight. I sat up and looked at myself. There was coolness in the morning air. My camel laid dejected not too far away. About me was a vast wasteland of broken country covered with rock and sand and thorny things. Not a sign of water. Not a piece of grain to eat for a person or beast.

" 'Could it be that in this peaceful quiet I face my end?' I told myself as my mind became clearer than ever before. My body now seemed of little importance. My parched and bleeding lips, my dry and swollen tongue, my empty stomach... all had lost their great agonies of the day before.

"I looked across into the uninviting distance and the question came to me once again, 'Have I the soul of a bonded servant or the soul of a free person?' Then with clearness I realized that if I had the soul of a bonded servant, I should give up, lie down in the desert, and die. A fitting end for a runaway bonded servant. But if I had the soul of a free person, what then? Surely, I would force my way back to Babylon, repay the people who had trusted me, bring happiness to my never forgotten spouse—who loves me truly, and bring peace and contentment to my parents.

" 'Your debts are your enemies who have run you out of Babylon,' Sira had said to me. Yes, it was so. Why had I refused to stand my ground like a person of pride? Why had I permitted my spouse to go back to their parents?

Then a strange thing happened. All the world seemed to be of a different color as though I had been looking at it through a colored stone which had suddenly been removed. At last, I saw the true values in life...

"Die in the desert? Not I! With a new vision, I saw the things that I must do. First, I would go back to Babylon and face every person to whom I owed an unpaid debt. I should tell them that after years of wandering and misfortune, I had come back to pay my debts as fast as the gods would permit. Next, I should make a home for my spouse and become a citizen who my parents would be proud of.

"My debts were my enemies, but the people I owed were my friends for they had trusted me and believed in me.

"I staggered weakly to my feet. What mattered, hunger? What mattered, thirst? *They were but the many inconveniences of life on the road to Babylon.* Within me surged the soul of a free person going back to conquer their enemies and reward my friends. I was thrilled with the great resolve.

"The glazed eyes of my camel brightened at the new note in my husky voice. With great effort, after many attempts, the beast gained its feet. With pitiful perseverance, we pushed on toward the north where something within me said we would find Babylon.

"We found water. We passed into a more fertile country where there was blessed grass and fruit. *We found the trail to Babylon because the soul of a free person looks at life as a series of problems to be solved and solves them, while the soul of a bonded servant whines, 'What can I do when I am but a bonded servant?'* "

***

"How about you, Tarkad?" Dabasir asked. "Does your empty stomach make your head most clear? Are you ready to take the road that leads back to self-respect? Can you see the world in its true color? Do you desire to pay your honest debts, however many there may be, and once again be a citizen respected in Babylon?"

Moisture came to Tarkad's eyes, and the youth rose eagerly to zir knees. "You have shown me a vision; already I feel the soul of a free person surge within me."

"But how fared you upon your return?" Questioned an interested listener to Dabasir.

"Where the determination is, the way can be found," Dabasir replied. "I now had the determination, so I set out to find a way. First, I visited every person to whom I was indebted and begged their indulgence until I could earn a coin to repay them. Most met me gladly. Several reviled me, but others offered a hand to help; one indeed gave me the very help I needed. It was Mathon, the gold lender. Learning that I had been a camel tender in Syria, Mathon sent me to old Nebatur, the camel trader, just commissioned by our Great Ruler of the City to purchase many herds of sound camels for the great expedition. Through Nebatur, my knowledge of camels I put to good use. Gradually I was able to repay every copper and every piece of silver. Then, at last, I could hold up my head and feel that I was an honorable citizen of Babylon."

Again, Dabasir turned to the plate of food, "Kushor, you fat snail of the desert!" Dabasir called loudly to be heard in the kitchen. "The food is cold. Bring me more fresh meat from the roasting. Then also bring a very large portion for Tarkad, the child of my old friend, who is hungry. They shall eat with me."

***

So ended the tale of Dabasir, the camel trader of old Babylon, who found their own soul when realizing a great truth—a truth that had been known and used by wise people long before this time.

This truth led people of all ages out of difficulties and into success and would continue to do so for those with the wisdom to understand its magic power. This power would be for any person to use who could read these lines,

Where the determination is, the way can be found.

WISE WORDS NEVER AGE

Parable 16

OCTOBER 21, 1934,

Dr. Keith Peyton

Care of the Carbondale Scientific Expedition in Hillah, Mesopotamia

Southern Illinois Normal University

Carbondale, Illinois

My Dear Professor:

The five clay tablets from your recent excavation in the ruins of Babylon arrived on the same boat as your letter. I have been utterly fascinated to no end and have spent many pleasant hours translating their inscription. I should have answered your letter at once but delayed until I could complete the translations which are attached.

The tablets arrived without damage, thanks to your careful use of preservatives and excellent packing.

You will be as astonished as we are in the laboratory at the story related in these tablets. One expects the dim and distant past to speak of romance and adventure. "Arabian Nights" sort of tales, you know? Instead, they disclose the problem of a person named

Dabasir paying off their debts. One realizes the conditions in this old world have not changed as much in 5,000 years as one might have expected.

It's odd, you know, but these old inscriptions rather humbled me, I must say. Being a college professor, I am supposed to be a human being, thinking and possessing a working knowledge of most subjects.

Yet, here comes this ancient figure from the dust-covered ruins of Babylon—offering a method I had never heard of to pay off my debts and at the same time acquire coins to jingle in my wallet.

It will be fascinating to prove if this plan works as effectively today as it did in ancient Babylon. Professor Keyserling and I are planning to try out this approach for our own affairs which certainly have room for improvement. Wishing you the best of luck in your worthy undertaking and eagerly awaiting for another opportunity to assist and converse.

Yours sincerely,

N. Keyserling

Department of Archaeology

Southern Illinois Normal University

Carbondale, Illinois

***

Tablet Number 1

Now, when the moons become full, I, Dabasir, having recently returned from bonded servantry in Syria, with the determination to pay my many just debts and become a citizen of means worthy of respect in my native city of Babylon, do hereby engrave upon the clay a permanent record of my affairs to guide and assist me in carrying through my high and noble desires.

Under the wise advice of my good friend Mathon, the gold lender, I am determined to follow an exact plan that is said to lead any honorable person out of debt and into self-sufficiency and self-respect.

This plan includes three purposes that represents my hope and desire.

First, the plan does provide for my future prosperity. Therefore, one-tenth of all I earn shall be set aside as my own to keep. For Mathon speaks wisely when they said:

That person, who keeps in their purse both gold and silver coins that are not to be spent, is performing a good deed for their family and their city.

That person, who has naught in their purse, is unkind to their family and bestows their weakness upon their city, for that person's own means and heart are bitter.

Therefore, the person who wishes to achieve, must ensure that they have kept coins to jingle in their purse, so that they have in their heart love for their family and loyalty to their city.

Second, the plan does provide that I shall still support and clothe my good spouse who has returned to me with loyalty from the house of their parents. For Mathon says that to take good care of a faithful spouse, puts self-respect into the heart of any person and adds strength and determination to their purposes.

Therefore, seven-tenths of all I earn shall be used to provide a home, clothes to wear and food to eat, with a bit extra to spend, so that our lives are not lacking in pleasure and enjoyment. But we must be forever diligent that we spend no greater than seven-tenths of what I earn for these worthy purposes. Herein lies the success of the plan.

For this is the mastery of the numbers, for which Mathon claims to bring any citizen of Babylon out of debt and into prosperity. I must live upon this portion and never use more, nor buy what I may not pay for out of this portion of seven-tenths. For the two-tenths are designated to pay off my debts and restore myself to honor. With one-tenths remaining to build for myself a future estate.

***

Tablet Number 2

Third, the plan does provide that out of my earnings, my debts shall be paid. Therefore, each time the moon is full, two-tenths of all I have earned shall be divided honorably and fairly among those who have trusted me and to whom I am indebted. Thus, in due time, all my indebtedness will be surely paid.

Therefore, do I here engrave the name of every person to whom I was indebted and the honest amount of my debt:

Fahru, the cloth weaver: 2 silvers, 6 coppers.

Sinjar, the couch maker: 1 silver.

Ahmar, my friend: 3 silvers, 1 copper.

Zankar, my friend: 4 silvers, 7 coppers.

Askamir, my friend: 1 silver, 3 coppers.

Harinsir, the jewel maker: 6 silvers, 2 coppers.

Diarbeker, my parent's friend: 4 silvers, 1 copper.

Alkahad, the house owner: 14 silvers.

Mathon, the gold lender: 9 silvers.

Birejik, the farmer: 1 silver, 7 coppers.

(From here on, the tablet had disintegrated and could not be deciphered.)

***

Tablet Number 3

To these creditors did I owe a total of 119 pieces of silver and 141 pieces of copper. Because I owed these sums and saw no way to repay, in my folly I did permit my spouse to return to their good parents and leave my native city to seek easy wealth elsewhere, only to find disaster and to see myself sold into the degradation of bonded servantry. Now that Mathon showed me how I could repay my debts in small sums of my earnings, did I realize the great extent of my folly in running away from the results of my extravagances. Therefore, I visited my creditors and explained to them that I have no resources with which to pay, except for my ability to earn, and that I intended to apply two-tenths of all I earned upon my indebtedness evenly and honestly. This much could I pay, but no more.

Therefore, if they were patient, in time my obligations would be paid in full.

Ahmar, whom I thought of as my best friend, reviled me bitterly and I left in humiliation.

Birejik, the farmer, pleaded that I pay zir first as the coin was badly needed.

Alkahad, the house owner, was indeed disagreeable and insisted that ze would give me trouble unless I did soon settle in full.

All the rest willingly accepted my proposal. Therefore, I became more determined than ever to carry on, being convinced it was easier to pay one's debts than avoid them. Even though I could not meet the needs and demands of a few of my creditors, I would deal impartially with them all.

***

Tablet Number 4

Again, the moon shines full. I have worked hard with a free mind. My good spouse has supported my intentions to pay my creditors. Because of our wise determination, I have earned during the past moon, by buying camels of sound wind and good legs, for Nebatur, the sum of 19 pieces of silver.

This amount I have divided according to the plan. One-tenth I have set aside to keep as my own, seven-tenths I have divided with my good spouse to pay for our living. Two-tenths I have divided among my creditors as evenly as could be done in coppers.

I did not see Ahmar but left what I owed with zir spouse. Birejik was so pleased with the coin, that I left with a kissed hand. Old Alkahad alone was grouchy and said I must pay faster. To which I replied, "If I were permitted to be well fed and not worried of reprisal, that alone would enable me to pay faster." All the others thanked me and spoke well of my efforts.

Therefore, at the end of one moon, my indebtedness was reduced by almost 4 pieces of silver, and I possessed almost 2 pieces of silver besides, upon which no other person could lay claim to. My heart was lighter than it had been for a long time.

Again, the moon shines full. I have worked hard but with poor success. I have been able to buy a few camels. Only 11 pieces of silver I have earned over these many nights. Nevertheless, my good spouse and I have stood by the plan even though we have bought no new raiment and eaten little but herbs.

Again, I paid myself one-tenth of the 11 pieces, while we lived upon seven-tenths. I was surprised when Ahmar commended my payment, even though it was small. So did Birejik. Alkahad flew into a rage, but when I was told to give back the portion owed to them, Alkahad did not wish it and became reconciled. The others, as before, were content.

Again, the moon shines full and I am greatly rejoiced. I intercepted a fine herd of camels and bought many sound ones; therefore, my earnings were 42 pieces of silver. This moon, my spouse and I have bought much-needed sandals and raiment. Also, we dined well on meat and fowl.

More than 8 pieces of silver we have paid to our creditors. Even Alkahad did not protest.

Great was this plan because it led us out of debt and gave us wealth that was ours to keep.

Three times the moon had been full since I last carved upon this clay. Each time I have paid myself one-tenth of all I have earned. Each time my good spouse and I have lived upon seven-tenths, even though at times, doing so was difficult. Each time, I have paid my creditors two-tenths.

In my purse I now have 21 pieces of silver that are mine. It makes my back straighten and makes me proud to walk among my friends. My good spouse keeps our home well and is becoming well settled.

This plan is of untold value. Has it not made an honorable citizen of Babylon out of an ex-bonded servant?

***

Tablet Number 5

Again, the moon shines full and I remember that it has been long since I carved upon the clay. Twelve moons have come and gone. But on this day, I will not neglect my record because on this day I have paid the last of my debts.

This is the day upon which my good spouse and I are thankful to celebrate with a great feast, for our determination has finally come to fruition.

Many things occurred, upon my final visit to my creditors, that I shall long remember. Ahmar begged my forgiveness for their unkind words and said I was the one above all others whom Ahmar wanted to be friends with.

Old Alkahad was not so bad after all, for ze said, "Thou was once a piece of soft clay to be pressed and molded by any hand that touched thee, but now thou are a piece of bronze capable of holding an edge. If thou need silver or gold at any time, come to me."

Alkahad was not the only one who held me in high regard. Many others spoke deferentially to me.

My good spouse looked upon me with light in zir eyes that would make a person have confidence in themself.

Yet it was the plan that made my success. It enabled me to pay all my debts and jingle both gold and silver in my purse. I did commend this plan to all who wished to go ahead. For truly, if it enabled an ex-bonded servant to pay their debts and have gold in their purse, would it not aid any person in finding independence? Nor am I, myself, finished with it, for I was convinced that if I followed it further, it would make me a rich citizen of this great city I call home. Babylon.

***

Dr. Keith Peyton

Care of the Carbondale Scientific Expedition in Hillah, Mesopotamia

Southern Illinois Normal University

Carbondale, Illinois

My Dear Professor:

If, in your further digging into those ruins of old Babylon, you encounter the ghost of a former resident, an old camel trader named Dabasir, do me a favor. Tell them that their scribbling upon those clay tablets, so long ago, has earned for them the lifelong gratitude of a couple of college folks back here in the States.

You will probably remember my writing a year ago that my spouse and I intended to try this plan for getting out of debt and at the same time having coins to jingle. You may have guessed, even though we tried to keep it from our friends, that we were in desperate financial straits.

We were frightfully ashamed for years of our old debts and worried sick, fearing that some of these creditors might start a scandal that would force me out of the college. We paid and paid, every penny we could squeeze out of our income. But it was hardly enough to halt the slow decline. Besides, we were forced to do all our buying where we could get further credit regardless of higher costs.

Our situation spiraled into one of those vicious circles that grew worse instead of better. Our struggles were getting hopeless. We could not move to less costly rooms because we owed the landlord. There did not appear to be anything we could do to improve our situation.

Then, here comes your acquaintance Dabasir, the old camel trader from Babylon, with a plan to do just what we wished to accomplish. This new friend stirred us up to follow this system enthusiastically. We made a list of all our debts, and I took it around and showed it to everyone we owed.

I explained how it was simply impossible for me to ever pay them for the way things were going along. They could readily see this for themselves from the figures I presented. I then explained that the only way I could pay in full was to set aside twenty percent of my income each month to be divided pro-rata, which would pay them in full in a little over two years. In the meantime, we would go on a cash basis and give them the further benefit of our cash purchases.

They were really quite decent. Our greengrocer, a wise old person, put it in a way that helped bring around the rest. "If you pay for all you buy and then pay some on what you owe," they said, "that is better than you have done, for you ain't paid down the account in three years." Finally, I secured all their names to an agreement binding them not to hound us as long as twenty percent of our income was paid regularly.

Then we began planning how to live upon seventy percent of our income. We were determined to keep that extra ten percent to jingle. The thought of earning that proverbial silver and gold was most alluring.

It was like having an adventure to make the change. We enjoyed figuring out this way and that, to live comfortably upon that remaining seventy percent. We started with rent and managed to secure a fair reduction. Next, we put our favorite brands of tea and such under suspicion and were agreeably surprised by how often we could purchase superior qualities at less cost.

It is too long of a story for a letter, but anyhow this adventure did prove no easy task. Still, we managed it—and quite cheerfully at that. What a relief it proved to have our affairs in such a shape we were no longer persecuted by past-due accounts.

I must not neglect, however, to tell you about that extra ten percent we were supposed to jingle. Well, we did jingle it for some time. Now don't laugh too soon. You see, that is the exciting part. It is really fun to start accumulating money that you do not want to spend.

There is more pleasure in running up such a surplus than there ever could be in spending it.

After we had jingled to our hearts' content, we found a more profitable use for our money. We took up an investment into which we could pay that ten percent each month. This has proven to be the most satisfying part of our regeneration. It is the first thing we pay out of our checks.

There is a most gratifying sense of security knowing our investment is growing steadily. By the time my teaching days are over, it should be a substantial sum. Large enough so the income will take care of us from then on.

All this came out of my same old check. Difficult to believe, yet absolutely true. All our debts are being gradually paid and at the same time our investment is increasing. We are getting along, financially, even better than ever before. Who will believe there can be such a difference in results between following a financial plan and just drifting along?

At the end of next year, when all our old bills have been paid off, we will have much more to pay toward our investment besides some extra for travel.

We are determined never again to permit our living expenses to exceed seventy percent of our income. Now, you can understand why we like to extend our personal thanks to that old citizen of Babylon whose plan saved us from our "Hell on Earth."

That Dabasir knew, because our ancestors of the past had been through it all. They wanted others to benefit from their own bitter experiences. That was why they spent tedious hours carving this message upon the clay. This person had a real message for fellow sufferers—a message so important that after five thousand years it had risen out of the ruins of Babylon, just as true and just as vital as the day it was buried.

Yours sincerely,

N. Keyserling,

Department of Archaeology

Southern Illinois Normal University

Carbondale, Illinois

WORK HAS GIFTED TO ME EVERYTHING I HAVE EVER HAD

Parable 17

AT THE HEAD OF THE CARAVAN proudly rode Sharru Nada, a merchant lord of Babylon. Ze liked fine cloth and wore rich and flattering robes. Ze liked fine animals and sat easily upon zir advanced years. Certainly, one would not have suspected that ze was inwardly troubled.

The journey from Damascus was long and the hardships of the desert were many.

The Arab tribes were fierce and eager to loot rich caravans. These looters showed no fear, so Sharru's fleet had to mount many guards and ze was well protected. The old merchant gave not a second thought to this.

About the youth at their side, on the other hand… this youth, traveling with them since Damascus, was rather disturbed. This was Hadan Gula, the grandchild of Sharru's business partner, Arad Gula, to whom Sharru felt a debt of gratitude was owed for which a humble person like themself could never hope to fully repay. Sharru would like to do something for this grandchild, but the more thought was put into the venture, the more difficult it seemed because of the youth's attitude.

Eyeing the youth's rings and earrings, Sharru thought, "Hadan thinks jewels are for them, but their grandparent never wore such gaudy robes. Yet, I asked Hadan to come, hoping I might help them get a start for themself and get away from the wreck their parent has made of their inheritance."

Hadan Gula broke in upon this thought, "Why do thou work so hard, riding always with thy caravan upon its long journeys? Do thou never take time to enjoy life?"

Sharru Nada smiled. "To enjoy life? What wouldst thou do to enjoy life if thou wert Sharru Nada?"

"If I had wealth equal to thy own, I would live like a sovereign. Never across the hot desert would I ride. I would spend the shekels as fast as they came to my purse. I would wear the richest of robes and the rarest of jewels. That would be a life of my liking, a life worth living." Both of them laughed together.

"Thy grandparent wore no jewels," Sharru Nada spoke in jest before thinking, then continued, "Wouldst thou leave no time for work?"

"Work was made for bonded servants," Hadan responded.

Sharru Nada bit zir lip and made no reply, riding in silence until the trail led them to a slope.

Here, Sharru reined zir mount and pointed to the green valley in the distance. "See, there is the valley. Look far down and thou canst faintly see the walls of Babylon. The tower is the Temple of Bel. If thy eyes are sharp, thou mayest even see the smoke from the eternal fire upon its crest."

"So, that is Babylon? Always have I longed to see the wealthiest city in all the world," Hadan Gula commented. "Babylon, where my grandparent started their great fortune. If ze was still here, we would not be so sorely pressed."

"Why wish a spirit to linger on this earth beyond its allotted time? Thou and thy parent canst well carry on their good work."

"Alas, of me and my parent, neither has that gift that made zir so special. We know not of this secret for attracting the golden shekels."

Sharru Nada did not reply but gently whipped the camel and they rode thoughtfully down the trail to the valley. Behind them followed the caravan in a cloud of reddish dust. Sometime later, they reached the Great Ruler of the City's highway and turned south through the irrigated farms.

Three old people plowing a field caught Sharru Nada's attention. They seemed strangely familiar. How ridiculous, ze thought.

One would typically not pass a field after forty years and find the same person plowing there. Yet, something within Sharru said they were the same. One, with an uncertain grip, held the plow. The others laboriously plodded beside the oxen, ineffectually beating it with their barrel staves to keep the beast pulling.

Oh! How, forty years ago, did Sharru envy these people? How gladly would ze have been to exchange places then? But what a difference now. Sharru Nada looked back with pride at the trailing caravan, with well chosen camels and donkeys, loaded high with valuable goods from Damascus.

Sharru pointed to the plowers and spoke to Hadan, "Still plowing the same field they were forty years ago."

"They look like it, but why do thou think they are the same?"

"I saw them there," Sharru Nada replied. Memories raced rapidly through their mind.

Why could these ghosts of the past not be buried in the past, Sharru thought, so life in the present could be appreciated? Then, Sharru saw, as in a painting, the smiling face of Arad Gula.

The barrier between zirself and the cynical youth beside zir dissolved.

How could a youth swaddled in a life of luxury hear the importance of words spoken from an old person?

Work could be offered in plenty to willing workers, but naught for a person who considered themself too good for work. Yet Sharru owed it to Arad Gula to do something to help their grandchild, and not just a halfhearted attempt. Sharru Nada and Arad Gula had never done things that way. They were not that sort of people.

A plan came in Sharru's mind almost in a flash, like lightning in the heavens. They had to take objections and cautions and consider their own family and standing. These would be cruel; these would hurt. But, being a person of quick decisions, ze waived away the inner objections and decided to act.

"Wouldst thou be interested in hearing how thy worthy grandparent and I joined in the partnership which proved so profitable?" Sharru proposed.

"Why not just tell me how thou made the golden coins? That's all I need to know," the youth parried with a sly grin.

Sharru ignored the reply and continued, "We start with those plowers of the field. I was no older than thou. As the column of people in which I marched approached, good old Megiddo, the farmer, scoffed at the slipshod way in which they plowed. Megiddo was chained next to me. 'Look at the lazy plowers,' ze said. 'The plow holder makes no effort to plow deep, nor do the beaters keep the oxen in the furrow. How can they expect to raise a good crop with poor plowing?' "

"Did thou say Megiddo was chained to thee?" Hadan Gula asked in surprise.

"Yes, with bronze collars about our necks and a length of heavy chain between us. Next to zir was Zabodo, the sheep thief. I had known zir in Harroun. At the end was a person called Pirate because they did not tell us their name. We judged them as a sailor as ze had entwined serpents tattooed upon their chest in sailor fashion. The column we marched in was four abreast."

"Thou was chained as a bonded servant?" Hadan asked incredulously.

"Did thy grandparent not tell thee I was once a bonded servant?"

"My grandparent often spoke of thee, but never hinted of this."

"Arad Gula was a person that can be trusted with great secrets. Thou, too, are someone I may trust, am I not right?" Sharru looked at Hadan squarely in the eye. With shoulders shrugging, Sharru said, "Any person may find themselves a bonded servant. It was a gaming house and barley beer that brought me disaster. I was the victim of my sibling's indiscretions. In a bar brawl, my sibling killed a friend. I was bonded to the widow by my parent, desperate to keep their first born from being prosecuted under the law. When my parent could not raise the silver to free me, the widow in anger sold me to the bonded servant merchant."

"What shame and injustice!" Hadan Gula protested. "But tell me, how did thou regain freedom?"

"We shall come to that, but not yet. Let us continue my tale."

***

"Long ago, I suspected those same plowers we just passed jeered at us. One removed their hat and did a little bow in mockery calling out, 'Welcome to Babylon, guests of the Great Ruler of the City. They wait for thee on the city walls where the banquet is spread, mud bricks and onion soup!' With that, they laughed uproariously.

“Pirate flew into a rage and cursed them roundly. I asked them, ‘What do those plowers mean by the Great Ruler of the City awaiting us on the wall?’

“ ‘To the city walls thou march to carry bricks until thy back breaks,’ responded Pirate. ‘Maybe they will beat thee to death before it breaks. They won’t beat me. I’ll kill ’em.’

“Then Megiddo spoke up, ‘It doesn’t make sense for them to talk of a master beating a willing, hard-working bonded servant to death. Masters like good bonded servants and treat them well.’

“ ‘Who wants to work hard?’ commented Zabodo. ‘Those plowers are wise fellows. They are not breaking their backs. Just doing enough to get by.’

“ ‘Thou cannot get ahead by shirking!’ Megiddo protested. ‘If thou plow a hectare, that’s a good day’s work and any master knows it. But when thou plow only a half, that’s shirking. I don’t shirk. I like to work, and I like to do good work, for the good work is the best friend I have ever known. It has brought me all the good things I’ve had: my farm and cows and crops, everything.’

“ ‘Yes, and where be these things now?’ scoffed Zabodo. ‘I figured it pays better to be smart and get by without working. Thou watchest me, Zabodo, if we’re sold to the walls. I will be carrying the water bag or some easy job when thou, who likes to work, wilt be breaking thy back carrying bricks.’ Zabado concluded laughing a silly trill.

“Terror gripped me that night. I could not sleep. I crowded close to the guard rope, and when the others slept, I attracted the attention of Godoso who was doing the first guard watch. Ze was one of those brigand Arabs, the sort of rogue who, if ze robbed thee of thy purse, would think ze must also cut thy throat.

" 'Tell me, Godoso,' I whispered, 'when we get to Babylon, will we be sold to the walls?'

" 'Why do thou want to know?'

" 'Can thou not understand?' I pleaded, 'I am young. I want to live. I don't want to be worked or beaten until death on the walls. Is there any chance for me to get a good master?'

"They whispered back, 'I tell thee something. Thou are good and give Godoso no trouble. Most times we go first to bonded servant market. Listen now. When buyers come, tell 'em thou a good worker, like to work hard for good master. Make 'em want to buy. Thou not make 'em buy thee, next day thou carry brick. Mighty hard work, for there are many bricks.'

"After Godoso walked away, I laid on the warm sand, looking at the stars and thinking about work. What Megiddo had said about it being a person's best friend made me wonder if it would grow to be my best friend in time.

"Certainly, it would be if it helped me out of this mess.

"When Megiddo awoke, I whispered my good news to zir. It was our one ray of hope as we marched toward Babylon. Late in the afternoon we approached the walls and could see the lines of people, like tiny ants, climbing up and down the steep diagonal paths. As we drew closer, we were amazed at the thousands of people laboring. Some were digging in the moat; others mixed the dirt into mud bricks. The greatest number were carrying the bricks in large baskets up those steep trails to the masons.

"Overseers cursed the laggers and cracked bullock whips over the backs of those who failed to keep in line. Poor, worn out people were seen staggering and falling beneath their heavy baskets, unable to rise again. If the lash failed to bring them to their feet, they were pushed to the side of the paths and left writhing in agony. Soon they would be dragged down to join the other craven withering bodies in the roadway to await unconsecrated graves. As I beheld the ghastly sight, I shuddered. So, this was what awaited me if I failed at the bonded servant market. This was motivation enough.

"Without letting on to the others, I slyly cleaned myself as good fortune only comes to those who are prepared to accept it, as they say.

"The famous works of old Babylon—its walls, temples, hanging gardens and great canals—were built by bonded servant labor, mainly prisoners of war, which explains the inhumane treatment they received.

"This workforce also included many citizens of Babylon and its provinces who had been sold into bonded servantry because of crimes or financial troubles. It was a common custom for people to put themselves, their spouses, or their children up as a bond to guarantee payment of loans, legal judgments, or other obligations. In case of default, those so bonded were sold into bonded servantry.

"Godoso had been right. We were taken through the city gates to the bonded servant prison and the next morning we marched as one to the pens in the market. Here, the rest of the people huddled in fear. Only the whips of our guards could keep them moving so the buyers could examine them. Megiddo and I eagerly talked to every person who permitted us to address them.

"The bonded servant dealer brought soldiers from the City Guard who shackled Pirate and brutally beat zir when ze protested. As the soldiers led the way, I felt only sorrow.

"Megiddo felt we would soon part ways. When no buyers were near, Megiddo talked to me earnestly to impress upon me how valuable work would be to me in the future. '*Some people hate it*,' ze said. '*They make it their mortal enemy. Better to treat it like a friend, make thyself like it. Don't mind because it is hard. If thou thinkest what a good house thou canst build, then who cares if the beams are heavy or the place is far from the well for carrying great amounts of water for the plaster?* Promise me, if thou get a master, work for them as hard as thou canst. If they do not appreciate all thou do, never mind it. Remember, work well done does good to the person who does it. It makes them a better person.' Megiddo stopped as a burly farmer came to the enclosure and looked at us critically.

"Megiddo asked about the farm and crops, soon convincing this farmer that ze would be a valuable bonded servant. After violent bargaining with the bonded servant dealer, the farmer drew a fat purse from beneath zir robe, and soon lucky Megiddo had followed zir new master out of sight.

"A few other people were sold during the morning. At noon, Godoso confided to me that the dealer was disgusted and would not stay over another night, but would take all who remained at sundown to a buyer working for the Great Ruler of the City's. I was becoming desperate when a fat, good-natured person walked up to the wall and inquired if there was a baker among us.

"I approached zir, saying, 'Why should a good baker like thyself seek another baker of inferior ways? Would it not be easier to teach a wiling person the skills of the trade? Look at me, I am young, strong, and like to work. Give me a chance and I will do my best to earn gold and silver for thy purse.'

"The baker was impressed by my willingness and began bargaining with the dealer, who never noticed me but now waxed eloquently on my abilities, good health, and good disposition. I felt like a fat ox being sold to a butcher. At last, much to my joy, the deal was closed. I followed my new master away, thinking I was the luckiest person in all of Babylon that night.

"My new home was much to my liking. Sibi, my master, taught me how to grind the barley in the stone bowl that stood in the courtyard, how to build the fire in the oven, and how to grind very fine the sesame flour for the honey cakes. I had a couch in the shed where the grain was stored. The old, bonded servant housekeeper, Swasti, fed me well and was pleased at the way I helped zir with the heavy tasks of the house.

"Here was the chance I had longed for to make myself valuable to my master and, I hoped, to find a way to earn my freedom.

"I asked Sibi to show me how to knead the bread and to bake. This ze did, much pleased at my willingness. Later, when I could do this well, I asked zir to show me how to make the honey cakes, and soon I was doing all the baking. My master was glad to be idle, but Swasti shook zir head in disapproval, saying, 'No work to do is bad for any person.'

"I felt it was time for me to think of a way by which I might start to earn coins of my own to buy my freedom. As the baking was finished by noon, I thought Sibi would approve if I found profitable employment for the afternoons and might share in my own earnings with me. Then the thought came to me: why not bake more of the honey cakes and peddle them to hungry people upon the streets of the city?

"I presented my plan to Sibi this way: 'If I can use my afternoons, after the baking is finished, to earn for thee coins, would it be only fair to share my earnings with thee so that I might have money of my own to spend for those things for which every person desires and needs?'

" 'Fair enough, fair enough,' ze admitted. When I told Sibi of my plan to peddle our honey cakes, ze was well pleased and said,

'Here is what we will do: sell them at two for a shekel, then half the shekels will be mine to pay for the flour and the honey and the wood to bake them. Of the rest, I shall take half, and thou shall keep half.'

"I was much pleased by this generous offer that I might keep for myself one-fourth of my sales.

"That night, I worked late to make a tray upon which to display the bread. Sibi gave me one of their worn robes that I might look presentable, and Swasti helped me patch it and wash it clean.

"The next day, I baked an extra supply of honey cakes. They looked brown and tempting upon the tray as I went along the street, loudly proclaiming my goods. At first, no one seemed interested, and I became discouraged. I kept on at it and later in the afternoon, as the people of the city became hungry, the cakes began to sell and soon, my tray was empty.

"Sibi was well pleased with my success and gladly paid me my share. I was delighted to own shekels. Megiddo had been right when ze said a master appreciated good work from their bonded servants.

"That night, I was so excited over my success, I could hardly sleep and tried to figure out how much I could earn in a year and how many years would be required to buy my freedom.

"As I went forth with my tray of cakes every day, I soon found regular customers. One of those was no other than thy grandparent, Arad Gula. Ze was a humble rug merchant and sold to the stay-at-home parents, going from one end of the city to the other, accompanied by a donkey loaded high with rugs and a blonde-haired bonded servant tending it. Ze would buy two cakes for themself and two for their bonded servant, always delighted to talk with me when they ate them.

"Thy grandparent said something to me one day that I shall always remember. 'I like thy cakes, but better still, I like the fine enterprise with which thou offer them. Such spirit can carry thee far on the road to success.'

"But how canst thou understand, Hadan Gula, what such words of encouragement could mean to a bonded servant? Lonesome in a great city, struggling with all the strength in zir to find a way out of this humiliation?

"As the months went by, I continued to add coins to my purse. It began to have a comforting weight upon my belt. Work was proving to be my best friend just as Megiddo had said. I was happy, but Swasti was worried.

" 'Our master is spending too much time at the gaming house,' Swasti told me, 'and I fear what may come of this.'

"One day, I was overjoyed to meet my friend Megiddo on the street. Ze was leading three donkeys loaded with vegetables to the market. 'I am doing mighty well,' I told Megiddo. 'My master does appreciate my good work, and for now I am a boss person. See, they do trust the marketing to me, and also, they are sending for my family. Work is helping me recover from my great troubles. Someday, it will help me buy my freedom and once more own a farm of my own.'

"Time went on and Sibi became more and more anxious for me to return from selling. Ze would be waiting when I returned and would eagerly count and divide our money. Ze would also urge me to seek further markets and increase my sales.

"Often, I went outside the city gates to solicit the overseers of the bonded servants building the walls. I hated to return to the disagreeable sights, but found the overseers liberal buyers. One day I was surprised to see Zabado waiting in line to fill zir basket with bricks. Zabado was gaunt and bent, and zir back was covered with welts and sores from the whips. I was sorry for zir and handed a cake, which was crushed into zir mouth like a hungry animal. Seeing the greedy look in zir eyes, I ran before ze could grab my tray.

" 'Why do thou work so hard?' Arad Gula said to me one day. I told zir what Megiddo had said about work and how it was proving to be my best of friends. I showed Arad with pride my wallet of shekels and explained how I was saving them to buy my freedom.

" 'When thou are free, what wilt thou do?' Arad Gula inquired.

" 'Then, I intend to become a merchant,' I said.

"At that, ze confided in me something I had never suspected. Thou do not know this, but I am also a bonded servant. I am in a partnership with my master.' "

***

"Stop," demanded Hadan Gula. "I will not listen to lies defaming my grandparent. Arad Gula was no bonded servant!" eyes blazing in anger.

Sharru Nada remained calm. "I honor thy grandparent for rising above their misfortune and becoming a leading citizen of Damascus. Are thou, their grandchild, cast of the same mold? Are thou strong enough to face true facts? Or do thou prefer to live under false illusions?"

Hadan Gula straightened in the saddle. In a voice suppressed with deep emotion, ze said, "My grandparent was beloved by all. Countless were their good deeds. When the famine came, did not Arad Gula's gold buy grain in Egypt and did not zir caravan bring it to Damascus and distribute it to the people so none would starve? Now, thou say they were but a despised bonded servant in Babylon?"

"Had ze remained a bonded servant in Babylon," Sharru Nada replied, "ze might well have been despised. But when, through their own efforts, Hadan Gula became a great citizen in Damascus, the gods indeed condoned this misfortune and honored them with respect."

***

Sharru Nada continued the story.

"After telling me they were also bonded servants, thy grandparent explained how anxious they had been to earn their freedom. After Arad had enough money to buy this great prize, ze was much disturbed as to what path one should take. They were no longer making good sales and feared to leave the support of their master.

"I protested this indecision. 'Cling no longer to thy master. Get once again the feeling of being a free person. Act like a free person and succeed like one! Decide what thou desirest to accomplish, and work will aid thee to achieve in it!' Upon hearing this, Arad went on their way saying they were glad I had shamed them for their cowardice.

"One day, I went outside the gates and was surprised to find a great crowd gathering there. When I asked a citizen for an explanation, their reply was, 'Has thou not heard? An escaped bonded servant who murdered one of the Great Ruler of the City's guards has been brought to justice and will this day be flogged to death for the crime. Even the Great Ruler will be here.'

"So dense was the crowd about the flogging post, I feared to go near lest my tray of honey cakes be upset. Therefore, I climbed up the unfinished wall to see over the heads of the people. I was fortunate to have a view of Nebuchadnezzar in the flesh as they rode in upon a golden chariot. Never had I beheld such grandeur, such robes and hangings of gold cloth and velvet.

"I could not see the flogging, though I could hear the shrieks of the poor bonded servant. I wondered how one so noble as our beautiful Great Ruler could endorse such suffering. And yet, when I saw ze was laughing and joking with the nobles, I knew ze was cruel and understood why such inhumane tasks were demanded of the slaves building the walls.

"After the bonded servant was dead, the body was hung upon a pole by a rope attached to their leg so all might see. As the crowd began to thin, I went close. On the hairy chest I saw, tattooed, two entwined serpents. It was Pirate.

"The next time I met Arad Gula, ze was a changed person. Full of enthusiasm I was greeted. 'Behold,' ze said, 'the bonded servant thou once knew is long gone, for I am now a free person! There was magic in thy words. Already my sales and my profits are increasing. My spouse is overjoyed. My spouse is a free person, the younger cousin of my master. My spouse much desires that we move to a new city where no citizen shall know I was once a bonded servant. Thus, our children shall be above reproach for their parent's misfortune. Work has become my best friend as thou once said. It enabled me to recapture my confidence and skill in selling.'

"I was overjoyed that I had been able to, even in a small way, repay Arad Gula for the encouragement ze had gifted to me."

***

"One evening," Sharru continued, "Swasti came to me in deep distress. 'Thy master is in trouble. I fear for them. For some months now they lost much at the gaming tables. Sibi does not pay the farmer for the grain nor for the honey. Ze pays not the money lender. They are all angry and making threats.'

" 'Why should we worry over their folly, we are not our master's keeper,' I replied thoughtlessly.

" 'Foolish youth, do thou not understand? To the money lender, thou wast given thy title of bonded servantry to secure a loan. Under the law, ze can claim thee and sell thee. I know not what to do. Sibi is a good master. Why? Oh why, should such trouble come upon zir?'

"Swasti's fears were not groundless. While I was doing the baking the next morning, the money lender returned with a bonded servant named Beltis. The lender looked me over and said I would do.

"The money lender waited not for my master to return but told Swasti to tell Sibi ze had taken me instead. With only the robe on my back and the purse of shekels hanging safely from my belt, I was hurried away from the unfinished baking by Beltis.

"I was whirled away from my dearest hopes as a storm tips over the mighty tree from the forest and casts it into the bog.

"Again, a gaming house and barley beer had caused me disaster.

"This Beltis was a blunt, gruff person. As they led me across the city, I told them of the good work I had been doing for Sibi and hoped to do good work for them as well. Beltis' reply offered no encouragement, 'I like not this work. My master likes it not. The Great Ruler of the City told them to send me to build a section of Grand Canal. Master tells Beltis to buy more bonded servants. Work hard and finish quick. Bah. How can any person finish big job quick?' "

***

"Picture a desert with not a tree. Just low shrubs and a sun that burned with such fury the water in our barrels became so hot we could scarcely drink it. Then imagine rows of people, going down into the deep excavation and lugging heavy baskets of dirt up soft, dusty trails from daylight until dark. Picture food served in open troughs from which we helped ourselves like swine. We had no tents, no straw for beds. That was the situation in which I found myself. I buried my wallet in a marked spot, wondering if I would ever dig it up again.

“At first, I worked with good will, but as the months dragged on, I felt my spirit breaking. Then the heat fever took hold of my weary body. I lost my appetite and could scarcely eat mutton and vegetables. At night I would toss in unhappy wakefulness.

“In my misery, I wondered if Zabado had not the best plan, to shirk and keep their back from being broken in work. Then I recalled my last sight of zir and knew that plan was no good.

“I thought of Pirate with their bitterness and wondered if it might be just as well to fight and kill. The memory of their bleeding body reminded me that this plan was also useless.

“Then I remembered my last sight of Megiddo. Zir hands were deeply calloused from hard work, but the heart was light and there was happiness on zir face. This plan seemed the best.

“Yet I was just as willing to work as Megiddo, and ze could not have worked harder than I. Why did my work not bring me happiness and success? Was it work that brought Megiddo happiness? Or are happiness and success just for the gods? Was I to work the rest of my life without gaining my desires, without happiness and success? All of these questions were jumbled in my mind, and I had not an answer. Indeed, I was sorely confused.

“Several days later, when it seemed I was at the end of my endurance and my questions still unanswered, Sibi sent for me. A messenger had come from my master to take me back to

Babylon. I dug up my precious wallet, wrapped myself in the tattered remnants of my robe, and was on my way.

"As we rode, the same thought relentlessly whirled in my fevered head like a storm lingering over a city. I seemed possessed, be living the strange words of a chant from my native town of Harroun:

'Besetting a person like a whirlwind,

Driving zir like a storm,

Whose course no one can determine,

Whose destiny no one can foretell.

Am I destined to be forever thus punished?

What new miseries and disappointments await me?'

"When we rode to the courtyard of my old master's house, imagine my surprise when I saw Arad Gula awaiting me. Ze helped me down my mount and hugged me like a long-lost sibling.

"As we parted ways from my old master's house, I would have followed Arad Gula as a bonded servant should follow the master, but Arad Gula would not permit me. Putting an arm around me, ze said, 'I hunted everywhere for thee. When I had almost given up hope, I did meet Swasti who told me of the money lender, who directed me to thy noble owner. A hard bargain did they drive and made me pay an outrageous price, but thou are worth every coin.' Continuing, 'Thy philosophy and enterprise have been my inspiration to this new success.'

" 'Megiddo's philosophy, not mine,' I interrupted.

" 'Megiddo's, yours, and now mine. We are going to Damascus, and I will need thee to be my partner. See! In one moment, thou wilt be a free person!' So saying, ze drew from beneath zir robe the clay tablets carrying my title. Arad Gula raised them above the head and hurled upon the stony ground to break them into a dozen pieces. With glee, we stamped upon the fragments until they were but dust."

***

"Still, to this day, tears of gratitude fill my eyes. I knew I was the luckiest person in Babylon. Work, thou see by this tale, in the time of my greatest distress, did prove to be my best friend.

"My willingness to work enabled me to escape from being sold to join the bonded servant gangs upon the walls. It also impressed thy grandparent, so much, ze selected me as their partner."

Then Hadan Gula questioned, "Was work my grandparent's secret key to the golden shekels?"

"It was the only key they had when I first knew of Arad Gula," Sharru Nada replied. "Thy grandparent enjoyed working. The gods appreciated the efforts and rewarded zir liberally."

"I begin to see," Hadan Gula spoke thoughtfully. "Work attracted the many friends who admired zir industry and the success it brought. Work brought to Arad Gula, the honors ze enjoyed so much in Damascus. Work brought them all those things I longed for. And I thought work was only fit for bonded servants."

"Life is rich with many pleasures for a person to enjoy," Sharru Nada commented. "Each has its own place. I am glad work is not reserved for bonded servants. Were that the case, I would be deprived of my greatest pleasures. Many things do I enjoy but nothing takes the place of work."

Sharru Nada and Hadan Gula rode in the shadows of the towering walls up to the massive, bronze gates of Babylon.

At their approach, the gate guards jumped to attention and respectfully saluted an honored citizen. With head held high, Sharru Nada led the long caravan though the gates and up the streets of the city.

"I have always hoped to be a person like my grandparent," Hadan Gula confided. "Never before did I realize just what kind of person ze was. This has been shown to me. Now that I understand, I do admire zir all the more and feel more determined to be like my grandparent. I fear I can never repay thee for giving me the true key to success. From this day forth, I shall use this key. I shall start humbly as my grandparent started, which befits my true station far better than jewels and fine robes." Then, reining zir horse, ze dropped back and rode with deep respect behind the leader of the caravan.

THE FOURTH DIMENSION

Parable 18

THERE ONCE WERE THREE FRIENDS who grew up within the same area of Babylon where many merchant families resided. These friends, for the most part of their childhood, spent time together and had a close friendship; they were almost inseparable, like woolen threads weaved tight together into a cloth ribbon.

Eventually, these friends went their separate ways but would still meet on certain occasions, like how a ribbon's woven threads would come loose in the middle but meet again at the end. One of them, a young adolescent named Dagan, thought of an idea ze believed could help them grow in their trades and make their bonds stronger.

"I have heard of a certain scholar in the city," Dagan said, "who is wise in the ways of coin and may have knowledge unconventional to many of us."

"Is this the wise Arkad you speak of?" Muranu, one of the friends, asked. "Ze has made a fortune that could rival many rich families in this great city."

Dagan shook the head. "Arkad may be wise and may be the richest person in Babylon. But I hear the scholar's wisdom exceeds that of this seasoned businessperson."

The third friend, Balasi, nodded. "Come to think of it, did we not hear that this eccentric scholar is a newcomer from a faraway land? Ze has only been here for less than a year, and people are saying their learning methods are unlike those used by the scribes of Babylon. We know the wise Arkad gained knowledge from formal institutions of learning, such as it is, and years of experience in trade. Still, we might learn from this intellectual some things not entirely known among many in this city. Perhaps, even unknown to the great Arkad themself."

"Then, my friend Balasi, I take it that you agree to go with me and see this scholar?" Dagan asked. "And what of you, Muranu? Only recently did you engage in trading. Some knowledge from them may be of benefit to your venture."

Muranu hesitated for a moment. "Dagan, I know you mean well when you proposed this idea to us. Still, we have heard little of the achievements of this peculiar sage you speak of. I shall go with you. But perhaps, I can speak with Arkad first? Ze might know something about this scholar, and it may be better to be informed before we proceed with this quest for knowledge, lest we receive ill advice and end up in dire straits."

Dagan frowned but understood Muranu's reservations. They agreed to meet again on the third day, the day they would visit the abode of the scholar.

At the agreed-upon day and time, Dagan and Balasi went together and headed for their destination. Muranu, who informed them the day before that ze might arrive late, suggested they meet at the scholar's house instead.

Upon their arrival at the house, which was close to the palace complex within the city, Dagan and Balasi went inside the doorless entrance and waited in the small, open-air courtyard in the middle of the abode. There, a middle-aged person in a long linen tunic approached them with a smile.

"I see one less of a group who, I was told, will visit me today," the person said. "Is that you, Dagan, child of Iddanim and inheritor to your family business of metalworkers?"

"It is indeed I, oh wise Tammuz," Dagan greeted with a bow. "And this is my companion and friend, Balasi, who comes from a line of stone carvers and architects. Their family was among those who worked on some of the great ziggurats and temples in this great city."

"How wonderful it is to hear of youngsters these days having a clear path to their crafts and trades. You are all well on your way to prosperity, should you keep up your pursuits." Tammuz the scholar paused. "If I am not mistaken, you have another companion joining us soon?"

"Our apologies for our tardiness," a voice from the entrance of the house said. "I am Muranu, an apprentice merchant in the business of trading goods like olives and grains. It is a pleasure to meet you."

Tammuz gazed at Muranu, and then at the older companion beside the young newcomer. "Now I see one more of the group who, I was told, will visit me today."

"My greetings to thee, Tammuz," Muranu's companion said, "and my thanks for making thy abode a welcoming place. I am Arkad, a friend of these three youths and one sought often for advice regarding matters of coin."

"Ah, wise Arkad, I have heard of you," Tammuz said. "Your renown as a successful businessperson and one whose fortune stands on top of Babylon has reached far and wide."

Arkad chuckled and made a soft smile. "There were rumors of a strange scholar in this city, but I did not bother learning anything of this person until young Muranu visited me. From there, I learned thou are a new resident here. A very wise yet unconventional person who spends all day thinking and earning their bread by answering questions for others. I thought, 'How novel.' And so, I decided to accompany these youths and see for myself how this person speaks."

Tammuz grinned. "You are here to test me, are you not? I understand your concern, for am I but a newcomer in your city, and you are unsure how the wisdom I can impart may be of use to these promising youngsters. Tell me, is there a particular topic you wish to know?"

"Muranu told me their group was interested in the concept of 'dimensions'—something they only heard of in passing when rumors about thee started to spread. At first, I did not understand what ze meant, and the first thing that came to my mind was one concerning measurements."

"We heard these 'dimensions' were referring to money," Muranu interjected, "or, at least, could be applied to matters concerning money. As young enterprising individuals, we thought such a concept may be interesting for our trades."

Once more, Tammuz smiled and was about to respond when ze looked toward the entrance of their house and noticed a couple of armed guards standing outside. Without a change in their expression, ze looked at Arkad and said, "Come, let us head to a more conducive place for learning."

Tammuz led the four guests into a back room illuminated through its window by the light from the open courtyard. On the wall to the right was a shelf containing many odd things, including a square cut stone. Tammuz grabbed the stone, which was as big as one's outstretched hand, and placed it on the table.

"You see," Tammuz began, "this rock has three dimensions. It has width," the scholar said, stroking their hand where the stone intersected the table. "It has height," ze continued while moving their hand up the side of the figure. "And it has length," ze said while running a finger on one side from front to back. "Although we, as humans, are not as simple as this stone, all things in this world have these three dimensions.

"However, there is a fourth dimension. All thinking beings know of it, but only a few can speak of and properly describe it.

"This dimension is time. It is like a mighty river. Always flowing one way and cannot be stopped. If you throw a stick into the river, the stick cannot go upstream. It can only go downstream. This stick can also only travel as fast as the river flows and not faster.

"Just like this stick, we cannot go backwards or forwards faster than time flows.

"But why you are here is to learn how this dimension relates to all of us. Well, let us look at this stone again. We have seen its three dimensions, but not the fourth dimension—time. For this stone is like the stick in the river, moving through time at a certain rate. The same rate as you and me.

"But we are educated beings. We know that if there is a single section of river, the water does not just stop when we can no longer see it or when it goes to places we have never seen before. The river will continue to flow. With no beginning and no end. Like time itself. We shall live by the grace of the gods in this city, but when we die, the river of time will still flow.

"Now, Arkad, I have been told thou are a wealthy person. Do many dispute this?"

"Only a few do," Arkad responded.

"Well, do you trust a stranger like me today? I know you have your guards outside my entryway as we speak. Will I be a fool to assume with a single shout from your mouth, they will charge in here to do your bidding?"

"It is as thou says."

"Then, you need not worry." With an outstretched arm, Tammuz pointed an open hand toward the table. "For me to explain the fourth dimension to all of you in a way that relates to your trade, I would like to ask the wise Arkad to please empty your purse here."

Arkad, with an amused look, did just that. Numerous gold, silver, and copper coins came out of the leather purse, clinking on the table and against each other in a small pile. The amount was more money than most living people would ever witness in their lives.

Even Dagan, Balasi, and Muranu, despite knowing Arkad as a rich person, still widened their eyes and dropped their jaws at this abundant number of coins on the table.

However, Tammuz did not seem impressed by the sight of these shining pieces of metal. With a look that remained unchanged since entering the back room, the scholar grabbed a gold coin like how one would pick up a dusty rock on the side of the road.

"Like the cut stone," Tammuz said, "this coin has dimensions. It has width, height, and depth. It also has time. If you were to invest this coin knowing its value will increase by, say, one-tenth annually, how much coin will you have at the end of the year?"

At first, Arkad thought whether this scholar was taking them for a fool. However, ze knew the answer and considered seeing the whole thing through. "One and one-tenth of a gold coin."

"Then, when you reinvest that entire amount, by the year's end your one and one-tenth of a gold coin shall increase by one-tenth more. Then the total shall be one and twenty-one-hundredths of a gold coin."

Arkad sighed. "Yes, I know my numbers and am aware of the concept of compounding interest. There is no magic or sorcery involved in this."

The scholar chuckled. "Now, now, my dear Arkad. I understand you are a rich person, perhaps the richest in all Babylon, and all of these things are likely not new to you. However, these young guests of ours are getting this knowledge for the first time. So, humor me for now, for you may discover something new still. Besides, you, among all other people I have met in this great city, are someone I expect to welcome wisdom, new and old. Am I a proper judge of your character?"

"My apologies if I may have come off as a little standoffish," Arkad said, their voice somewhat softer this time. "These youngsters seemed to have placed thee on a pedestal, and in my overestimation, I closed my mind to the wisdom I already learned. Very well, I shall, for a moment, revert my mind to that of a student and consider thee my teacher. Based on thy example, from the way my principal grew, I should expect to receive around one and one-third of a gold coin by the third year."

"A wise realization, and a correct conclusion," Tammuz said. "Then, for clarity, I shall show you the amounts in estimates of what you can get up to the tenth year."

Tammuz then sat on a chair, grabbed a reed stylus, pulled a wet clay tablet on the table toward themselves, and began writing the following figures on the tablet.

Year 1: 1 gold + 1/10 interest = 1.10 gold
Year 2: 1.1 gold + 1/10 interest = 1.21 gold
Year 3: 1.21 gold + 1/10 interest = 1.33 gold
Year 4: ... 1.46 gold
Year 5: ... 1.61 gold
Year 6: ... 1.77 gold

Year 7: ... 1.94 gold
Year 8: ... 2.14 gold
Year 9: ... 2.36 gold
Year 10: ... 2.59 gold

After writing these figures on the clay tablet, Tammuz presented them to Arkad and the three youths. "This is the fourth dimension of a gold coin when profitably invested. Growth. As a rich person, you, Arkad, have a great many coins earning more coins, and I am sure all of them will continue this cycle for many years to come.

"As for you three youngsters, seek an investment that will make your coins grow in value over time. Do not let your coins stay trapped in their physical forms with three dimensions only. Bring them to the fourth dimension, a dimension that flows without stopping. If you are wise, think of the coins' value as it is today and as it will be in the future. Think of the opportunity for growth each coin has.

"Now, suppose you go your separate ways today and in the third year, you meet each other again. Then, you decide to have a small feast to celebrate your reunion... and perhaps, impress each other as well. Instead of growing your coin by one-tenth more, you decide to spend one-tenth of the gold you have thus far for this occasion.

"And so, you and your companions gather and have plenty of food and wine in celebration of your friendship. Then, after the festivities are over, you decide that for the next seven years, you will faithfully reinvest your gold. In this case, how much will you have by the tenth year if you consistently earn one-tenth of your accumulated coin annually?"

Dagan gazed upon the figures on the wet clay tablet. "Each of us should have two and thirty-six-hundredth gold coins by then, the same amount we could have earned in the ninth year had we not spent on the feast."

The scholar nodded. "There are wise people in Mesopotamia who call this difference in outcomes as the opportunity cost. The coin you spend today will cost you coins you could have earned in the future, for you missed an opportunity to invest these coins to their full potential. It is as if time stopped for these coins during the period you did not invest them.

"Imagine if all citizens of your city thought of the opportunity cost of their purchases?" Tammuz laughed. "Of course, one must buy bread to eat and wine to drink, and one cannot wear the same tunic every day until it turns into a rag, lest they want to appear like beggars. But aside from these necessities, if the people denied themselves earthly pleasures today and built up their wealth for tomorrow, imagine the great liberality they might enjoy in the future."

"This concludes my lesson on dimensions." Tammuz took a moment to look at each of the guests before continuing. "Remember that each coin you take from your purse to spend today takes away part of that coin's opportunity for future growth. Like all things in this mortal world, a coin exists in four dimensions. As you increase your skill and experience through time, so can your coin grow in value."

"And where should we invest our coins," Muranu asked, "so that we may enjoy their growth in the fourth dimension?"

Tammuz smiled and looked at Arkad, who seemed to have become agreeable with the scholar. "That question, my young friend, is better answered by the richest person in Babylon."

YOUR ARMY, BOUGHT WITH THEIR COIN

Parable 19

ATOP THE SACRED WALLS OF BABYLON sat a young captain of the City Watch. Deep in thought while viewing the horizon with a blank stare as the afternoon sun shone on zir face, ze did not notice any soldier approaching until ze felt a modest pat on zir back.

"A spy or assassin may have snuck up here," a soldier, a sergeant of an age older than the captain, said, "and whatever deep thoughts thou has at this moment will all have been slain together with thee."

"My good sergeant," the captain said, voice firm but with a slight crack, "such is not the proper way to approach me. I outrank thee, and thou would be wise to exercise protocol, whether in peace or war."

"The enemy will not care for such civilities, captain. As a sergeant, I want my soldiers, even my officers, to be of strong bodies and keen minds. And yet, that look of distraction on your face could have cost you your life."

The sergeant paused, but the captain only sighed and gave no response.

"Pray tell," the sergeant continued, leaning closer to the captain, "what bothers thee so strongly that thou will exchange vigilance for momentary carelessness atop these hallowed walls?"

The captain pursed zir lips. "To be brief, I worry whether my purse will last another week. My spouse is a garment merchant and we pool what money we set aside for our family. By some misfortune, the caravan bringing my spouse's merchandise was raided by bandits a week ago. My spouse believes we can recover the merchandise, but I am unsure if we can do so."

The sergeant ruffled zir beard. "Suppose this merchandise you speak of shall no longer be recovered and profits from it no longer realized. Will this misfortune bring ruin to your family?"

A sudden reflection crossed the captain's mind and for a moment went silent. Crossing zir arms and gathering zir wit, the captain responded, "I do not believe so."

"And why is that?"

"As a soldier of the Great Ruler's army, I still earn my wage. And as a captain, truth be told, my earnings are enough—and a bit more—to support my household."

"In other words," the sergeant said, smiling, "the Great Ruler's army will still provide for your needs! Your family still has food on the table. Your arms still have a sharp spear and a sturdy shield. Your body still has tunic and armor. You shall remain provided. And if you are wise enough, you can even support your spouse's business with the coin you save.

"My young friend, you may be my captain, but I have the wisdom of age. You must 'bend your mind,' as those travelers from the Far East say. You see money as something that can buy a leg of a goat or a tunic. But money can be used for far more than that.

"Pray tell, what is the most inexpensive way to build an army? Do you know of one? Each soldier must have good armor and a strong spear. They must have a place to sleep and good food to eat to preserve their strength. And with an army in the thousands , the daily upkeep boggles the mind. So, how can one do it? By being wise in the way of money.

"Have you ever wondered why Great Rulers of Cities have their faces stamped on a coin and circulated among their subjects? This is the easiest way to build an army or a great city. Instead of running the royal treasury dry, the Great Ruler can put their coin into the hands of their army, such as one comprising ten thousand strong people. This army then demands each citizen of the cities they protect to pay the Great Ruler of the City one coin per moon, even though the Great Ruler never gave a single citizen any of these coins.

"This action turns the city's economy into one focused on relieving the soldiers of their newly given coins. Now each family, in order to get their hands on these coins, must find some way to contribute to the war effort by providing soldiers with things soldiers value, such as straight spears, strong camels, and good food.

"This is why rulers consult those with the wisdom to make and use coins for their advantage. It is common knowledge among these elites that the creation of new taxes, payable in certain coins, is far more convenient for paying an army. But this creation is also useful in many other ways because it means officials no longer have to purchase everything they need directly from the people or royal workshops."

Hearing these words, the captain once again stared at the horizon but with renewed hope this time. As long as ze was wise in the ways of the coin as the Great Ruler of the City was, zir family would be well-provided as much as the army provided for them and still have opportunities to bounce back despite the momentary financial setback.

THE EQUATIONS OF WORK

Parable 20

YALA, a spirited youth who lived near an area of the city where freepeople resided, walked at a brisk pace one morning toward the courtyard house of Balto, a well-known merchant in Babylon. As usual, there was a small crow near the public candles that told which hour of the day it was. Upon Yala's arrival, ze saw the elderly merchant preparing a camel loaded with various goods to head for the market.

"Elder Balto!" Yala shouted, running toward Balto before the merchant could leave. "May I indulge you in a morsel of good news?"

"Ah, Yala, full of energy, as usual," Balto said, laughing. "So, what news do thou have for me?"

"This morning, a palace scribe praised me for doing well in my arithmetic," Yala said with a full grin. "They said I learned more than what many other students my age did. It's all thanks to your tutelage!"

"That is excellent news, indeed." Balto patted the camel and turned to the cameleer behind the animal. Balto then gave instructions to the cameleer and sent zir and the camel off, leaving Balto alone with Yala. "Then, I believe thou are here for the promised reward, are thou not?"

Yala tapped zir fists twice on zir chest. "The people of Babylon indeed speak the truth when they say you always keep your promises. Then, I am here for that exact purpose."

"Very well, young Yala. If it is within my capacity, I shall grant thy reward. Tell me what it is thou do seek."

Humming and with crossed arms, Yala took a while to come up with an idea. "I have always been curious. Under whose trade are you working for?"

" 'Working for?' " Balto shook zir head. "I own the business. Have thou not noticed after all this time thou have visited me in my abode? I work not for anyone."

"I don't understand," Yala said with furrowing eyebrows. "Is your job not similar to a manager who works for an employer?"

Balto rolled zir eyes. "Thou may do well in thy academics, but it appears thou are in need of further wisdom when observing people and business. I am no foreman or supervisor who 'manages' a company. Unlike such positions, mine does not entail working for someone else."

"If so," Yala continued, "what does it mean to be an owner of a business?"

Sensing Yala's vexation slowly turn into a growing sense of interest, Balto calmed zir breath and cleared zir throat. "If thou wish to learn what being a proprietor is, first, let us talk about the philosophy of work, my young friend," ze smiled. They both went to the front of Balto's house and sat on some chairs, with the crowded street a few arm lengths away.

"A worker employed in a business gives up hours for the service of someone else. Each of us has a parade of days in this world, and a worker exchanges these days for a wage. This employer sells the worker's service to someone for more money than the worker's wages. Thus, the employer values that service higher than the wage they pay to the worker. This is how a normal business runs.

"Some believe a business is healthy when the worker and employer, receiving a suitable income from the services the workers render, are both able to prosper. Whereas an unhealthy business... thou can describe it as a venture where the worker is not receiving a living wage yet the employer is receiving a high revenue. But this branch of philosophy can wait for another time.

"Now the manager does not actually do the specific service that generates the income. Ze directs the business in a way that is profitable. This can come in many different forms. I think it is best to think of a manager as a master of a naval ship. The master steers the ship to where it needs to be to generate income, but the ze does not do the actual work of setting the sails, pumping the bilges, or scrubbing the decks. Ze just directs the flow of the ship. So, a manager can direct the flow of supplies into the business, steer the business into profitable endeavors, and ensure a steady workforce to do the services that creates income for the business.

"On the other hand, an owner of the business has a hands-off relationship with the enterprise. Of course, owners are humans, and humans like to be in charge of things, so they can pick the direction the company is going. Yet, the owner has no direct input into the service performed to make money for the company.

"Many believe the owner is the best position in a business, because ze needs not to perform any work there and yet is entitled to a portion of the profits. Sounds pretty nice, right? Going back to our little naval analogy, the owner would be the captain's commanding officer. What's interesting about this officer is that they often do not have seagoing experience and do not even need to sail with the ship. Instead, ze simply tells the master which way the ship should go. The master manages the crew, and the crew does the actual work that keeps the boat moving.

"Now let us look at a small business. Thou may have other ways to call it, such as a sole proprietorship, a self-employed person, or one who self-defines themselves as 'I own a small business.' Imagine a person who bakes bread and sells it. Ze owns zir business and thus is entitled to the profits, but ze also must work and manage the shop as well. Buying flour or grinding grain, baking bread, selling it, accounting, and acquiring new customers, the endless cleaning... these are essential for the business to prosper.

"One can say a person who is self-employed owns nothing more than their job. What I mean is, that person still fills the role of a worker, for they provide a service that is purchased. Since they are their own boss, they need to have more capacity, more room to maneuver, for handling the direction, hours, and scope of work they perform. But one cannot forget that for the business to make an income, this 'owner of the small business' must actually do the work.

"As for a business with multiple people doing work, it will generate revenue without having the owner do any work at all. If thou have heard of the phrase 'they own their job,' this concept is where that saying comes from.

"But think of this, my young friend. If this sole proprietor angers the gods and they are punished by a broken finger or the yellow sickness, how will the business run? If the small business owner does all the work in the business, then the business only makes coin while they are working in it. So the small business is, in reality, only as prosperous as the body of the owner. Because once they grow ill, the business now grows ill and makes no coin."

Upon hearing this lengthy lecture, Yala folded zir arms and

placed the back of one hand under zir chin. Seeing this gesture, Balto paused and waited for Yala to speak up first.

"If that is so," Yala said, breaking the silence, "Why does it seem some workers are not as prosperous as the owner if they, as you say, own their job? And why do some owners look like they are doing more than what they should despite having workers under their employ?"

"These things may happen," Balto replied, "when the business shows signs of being unhealthy. Some people will look at this and call it a 'rat race.' Thou see, when thou do put a rat in a wheel, and the creature runs and runs inside it, the wheel turns but the rat goes nowhere.

"This is why it is wise for a sole proprietor to set up and run a business without providing direct service to the customer. To say it in different words, the entrepreneur who started the business should transition out of the worker role and into the owner role. So that the owner can be in a position to receive income without doing the services a worker does to propel the business.

"So, Yala, I shall say it again. I am no worker but a business owner. Does that answer thy question?"

"I can now see the difference, yes," Yala answered with a nod.

"Now," Balto continued, "since thou do pick up concepts quite quickly, and I am pleased with thy progress, I shall bestow upon thee another piece of knowledge thy peers at school are unlikely to gain soon. Tomorrow, bring me a stick, twice as long as thy arm. Meet me here in this house again in the third hour after noon and we shall walk to the Euphrates."

And so, Yala did as Balto instructed. On the next day, Yala returned to Balto's residence and headed to the shore of the great river.

"So, Yala," Balto said as they walked along the riverbank, "thou have had the night to think about what we spoke of yesterday. What say thee of that topic?"

"It was enlightening," Yala began. "You taught me what makes a business owner and how their job differs from that of a hired hand. And while owners, like the so-called sole proprietor, can do what a worker does, an ideal enterprise should be one where the owner does no direct work and the worker performs the actual services. A proper balance of responsibilities between these roles should enable the business to prosper and be healthy."

Balto smiled and clapped zir hands once. "Ah, yes, very well said. Now let us discuss what I like to call the equations of work.

"For most people alive today, they give their hours to receive an income. That is to say, they prefer to receive their daily income based on the number of hours worked in a day and how much they make in an hour. May I borrow that stick, Yala?"

"Of course," Yala said, handing the stick to Balto by the other end.

"Should thou do put that in an equation, it should look like this..." Balto then started scribbling something on the sand.

$$\textit{Hours Worked} \times \textit{Wage} = \textit{Income}$$

"So, in this equation," Balto said, "there are two ways to increase thy income. Thou shall increase thy wage, which most people have little ability to do, or increase thy hours. Which most people can do, but there are limits to our bodies. Most people turn ill if they work for more than a day straight without taking a break. So, in this equation, it is realistic for someone young and healthy to work twice as many hours... but it is unrealistic for anyone to triple their hours. So, this equation has limits.

"Suppose thou are a humble cloth merchant, who walks the streets of Atlantis or Babylon selling garments out of the saddlebags of thy donkey. Thy equation should, therefore, look like this..."

Below the previous equation drawn on the sand, Balto wrote the following.

Cloth Sold × (Price of Cloth - Cost of Materials) = Income

"Thou see in this example that there is no correlation to the worked hours or set wage," Balto said as ze began writing another line below. "The cloth merchant can make as much or as little money as they want. But there is also no hard limit to what they can earn. Now, think of an employed bricklayer who gets paid by the hour. Assuming ze works the entire day, from sunset to sunset, thou can compute the most they can earn as..."

24 Hours × Wage = Income

Yala squinted zir eyes at this new equation scribbled on the sand and shook zir head. "But bricklayers cannot work those kinds of hours for long, can they?"

"Ah, thou are finally seeing it," Balto said. "Compare that to the cloth merchant, who may sell five clothes one day and meet a rich person who buys one hundred clothes the next day.

"This income based on the sales is what I call a dynamic income. It is not tied down to the hours on the clock that thou must commit to the task of earning. Rather, this income is based on results.

"These equations thou sees on the sand revolve around a worker providing a service for someone. Now, let me show thee something else. Consider the wage of a scribe. Suppose they spend a fixed amount of time, let us say ten hours, crafting a story, an epic, and writing it on clay tablets and receive a dynamic income for the rest of their lives based on those ten hours of work. Can thou figure out their income through this..."

Balto moved to the side and, in another column beside the equations on the sand, ze wrote a new line.

1 Hour Work × Sales = Income

"This fascinates me, so I beg many pardons for repeating myself," Balto said, raising the stick and, with a smug face, tapping the stick on Yala's shoulder. "But by putting in even just a single hour of work, a scribe, whose work will likely last a lifetime, as words do not age like crops. They can receive an income for the rest of their life from that one hour.

"See how different this is from the bricklayer who receives one unit of wage for every hour of work? There is no magic or sorcery in this equation. This is how thinkers and inventors often become wealthy. By devoting a year of their life to bringing a product to market, they then receive an income after that years' worth of work for decades to come."

A wide-eyed Yala was silent for a moment, and Balto giggled at the youngster's jawdropped expression. Balto waited until Yala appeared to have gotten the concept, after which Yala nodded with a generous grin.

"I can sense some satisfaction on thy face," Balto teased. "Shall we examine another example, then? This time, at the income of a lender of coin. Or, as some may call them, an investor. When they invest their money, that amount becomes the principal or capital. By lending out this principal, they receive a rental, dividend, or interest, which is a percentage of the total principal.

"So, young Yala, if the lender invests a hundred gold coins and expects a return of one-tenth of that amount per year, what will the equation look like?"

Yala tilted their head and looked down on the sand. "I guess the solution is something like..."

When Yala looked at Balto, the wise elder knew what the youth wanted to do. Balto then gave the stick to Yala, who proceeded to scribble on the sand below the last equation Balto wrote.

$$(\,100\ Coins \times (1/10)\,) + 100\ Coins = 110\ Coins$$

"Thy lines are a little crooked but readable enough," Balto said. "Can thou tell me how thou came up with this?"

"From what I understood," Yala began, "the lender gets the hundred gold coins back plus one-tenth of that principal. Since one-tenth of a hundred is ten, this amount is added to the principal as the interest payment."

Smiling, Balto then asked, "Oh my! Thou are a wise one! And what else did thou do notice?"

Yala narrowed zir eyes. "The equation... does not consider the sales or hours of work?"

"Well observed!" Balto praised. "The most important work an investor does is finding a safe investment for their money, then the money does the work for them.

"Now, let us look at one final equation, and that is the equation of the owner. As we said before, the owner receives revenue despite not directly doing the actual service or managing all parts of the business to keep it operational. The most they may do is pick the course of the business in one direction or another, like how a commanding officer leads a ship. And so, the owner's equation is as follows..."

Once more, Yala handed the stick to Balto, who wrote a new line —and in bigger symbols—below all the other equations on the sand.

Revenue = Income

"Look at that!" a beaming Balto said. "The owner receives an income separate from their hours."

"Now I understand why you decided to be a business owner," Yala said. "You invested coin to set up your business, hired workers, instructed them as to how you want your business to go, then paid them by the hour. Meanwhile, you receive income while being hands-off. Truly, even as we speak and walk along the Euphrates, you are still earning coin!"

Balto gave a hearty laugh, like a merchant who sold all their goods in a morning to a rich person. "Not many people are aware of this knowledge. And now that thou have learned of it, I hope thou shall become prosperous and wise in the ways of money from today until the end of days!"

A WALKING PARABLE

Parable 21

A FOREIGNER who would set foot in Ancient Babylon should not be fooled by its towering walls and buildings of mud and clay. For behind these structures existed numerous industries that helped build its civilization.

In the heart of many of these industries were prominent merchant families that traded not only within but outside Babylon. Often in these families, members engaged in various trades. One parent could be the head, one child could be a metalworker, a sibling could be selling textiles in the city, and a cousin could be trading oils and other goods in Egypt.

In other words, each family member could pursue a different industry and needed not to be in the same trade as other members and relatives.

However, a young adolescent named Shamash, a member of one such merchant family, seemed to find this dynamic difficult to handle. Born as the third child, Shamash had little prospect when it came to inheriting the family business. This thought left them at a fork in the road as to what industry to pursue should ze someday live on their own, without the support of a family.

At first, Shamash tried various trades. Ze once pursued farming but realized it did not interest them. Ze then tried pottery, even training under Amurum, a well-known craftsperson in Babylon. But Shamash was not engrossed in the idea of getting caked in mud and clay every day. Shamash even considered helping their parent sell garments and other textiles, but ze lacked the proficiency to negotiate with customers, especially those who bought in bulk or had a discerning eye for fabric quality and details.

Soon, Shamash realized ze wasted several years trying out things without settling on a specific trade or craft. Ze could not help but compare zirself to other peers of their age and younger, many of whom seemed to succeed in their pursuits and specialties.

That thought made their chest feel heavy. Knowing their other siblings were successful in their own industries, Shamash did not speak of this conundrum to their parents, who ze assumed might express disappointment if they knew.

Burdened by this contemplation, the young fellow one day lumbered down the streets of Old Babylon. Shamash hung their head low and their leather sandals made heavy dragging sounds on the uneven pavement. Every step ze took was shaky and reminded zir of the failures ze had in life.

This string of misfortunes made Shamash unable to shake the feeling that some invisible force was determined to keep them down, turning every hope into dust. Despite their countless efforts, Shamash still felt success always seemed out of reach. The bustling street, usually filled with laughter and chatter, felt distant and uncaring.

As the youth rounded a corner on a busy street on their way home, ze stumbled upon a familiar wise person. The student approached them and asked, "Teacher, it is I, Shamash, the child of Samri. Do you remember me?"

"Shamash..." the teacher, Beltis, repeated in a low, fading voice. After a moment, ze beamed with a smile that reached to their ears. "Ah, I remember thee, my young student! My, thy expression has not changed, despite thy height being a half-foot taller since I last saw thee in my lectures."

"I am glad you remember me, teacher. Your wise counsel has often been of great significance to us at school. Among the scribes and other teachers, you are one of those we students find most helpful, and we learned plenty from you."

Beltis laughed. "I would like to thank thee. But for some reason, the way thou flatter me seems distant from what thou truly desire. As it was back then, thy face seems full of trouble. Ah, could it be that thou encountered some sort of predicament?"

"Your intuition is as impeccable as it was back then, wise teacher." Shamash sighed and clasped both hands before them. "Why do I have such bad luck finding success in life? I see people younger than me surpassing me. Why do the gods hate me so?"

Amused by the youth's frankness, Beltis replied, "Did thou approach me to learn or have thy question answered?"

Shamash hesitated, thinking twice about how to answer that question. But ze thought there might be little chance for them to meet the teacher again. So, after a brief pause, the student shook their head and, with a determined look on the face, responded, "To learn."

"Very well. Come with me." Beltis placed a hand on Shamash's shoulder and together they walked to a less crowded place, for the corner of the street where they met was full of noise and chattering people that a scholarly lecture would be counterproductive.

They arrived at a quiet garden and sat in a small alcove on a nearby wall. Here, the trees and buildings muted the clamor on the streets.

"Now, tell me, Shamash, child of Samri," Beltis said, "do thou still maintain thy company with Balto and... Lyar, was it?"

"Yes, I do, each night after work," Shamash replied.

"What often do you talk about?"

"Elder Balto would talk of their travels, especially those in foreign lands. Ze would tell stories of their experience in trading goods of silver and gold, of stone and lumber, and even of textiles and leather. Ze would tell stories of clients young and old, rich ones and stingy ones, and freepeople and bonded servants."

"And of Lyar? What did ze speak about?"

Shamash took a deep breath. "Lyar... is a thief. It is known and ze has had plenty of confrontations with the law. Ze would often argue with Balto, and Balto would be inconvenienced because of Lyar. In turn, I would end up getting in trouble, for while Balto would speak words of wisdom regarding trade, Lyar would dismiss them, and I would get discouraged. I never have had a fruitful discussion when these two are together!"

Beltis nodded. "I see thy predicament, but this is no fault of the gods. Rather, thou are receiving advice, both wise and ill, from widely different kinds of people, and so thou end up with neither," Beltis said. "From how I see it, thy time spent with them hampered more than helped thee in finding thy direction and purpose."

Shamash dropped their shoulders and sighed once more. "As the third child, I am not as pressed for greatness and achievement as my older siblings are. But if I keep moving at a snail's pace while being beset by the people around me, I will soon find myself gathering the dust left by my peers and even those younger than me."

These words, within a moment of thought, compelled Beltis to help a former student as the teacher now knew what this young fellow needed. Beltis stood and told Shamash, “Let us walk, for I will show thee something thou must learn.”

The two left the alcove and strolled back into the streets of Babylon. Although Beltis was no longer as nimble as the young student due to age, the teacher kept up a brisk pace, walking beside Shamash and faster than most in the crowd.

After passing a couple of blocks in silence, Beltis slowed down and walked at nearly half the pace of the crowd trudging past them through the street. Shamash, puzzled by this action, also eased down their pace but kept their questions within their lips. When a good number of people had overtaken them, the teacher resumed a normal pace.

The pair walked past several more blocks, with Beltis changing their pace a couple more times and Shamash matching the speed, before turning toward an alley. Soon, the pair found themselves in another small garden. The silence once more drowned out the cacophony of the people.

The teacher stopped and turned to face the student. “Now, young Shamash, did thou observe anything as we walked?”

“I noticed you kept changing your pace, teacher. You walked fast at one point, then slow, then moderately, then fast again. I almost stumbled twice trying to keep up and then slow down.”

“So, thou have noticed,” Beltis said, smiling again as ze looked at the youth. “My student, when I said we would walk, I did not tell thee to keep up and walk beside me. And yet thou did without being told to do so. When I sped up, thou did as well. When I slowed down, thou matched my pace.

“Look outside this alley, at the multitude of life passing through that street. Notice how the crowds of people walk at their own speed, each individual walking just as fast as the rest of their group? Humans, for reasons only the gods know, seem to walk at the same speed as those around them.

"Now, think about those people with whom thou spend thy time —the wise merchant Balto and the troublesome thief Lyar. Do they inspire success in thee? Do they go out of their way to help thee achieve thy goals? Or do they only live for the day, without regard for tomorrow?

"Perhaps, if Lyar had wisdom unbeknownst to many, thou might have learned from him as much as thou could have with Balto. A thief could tell thee when to talk and when to keep silent, when to run and when to fight. Ze could say when to go to a high place and when to go low. Ze could talk about who to take from and who to leave alone.

"You could have been wise in the ways of trade through Balto, and wise in the ways of the streets through Lyar. But alas, thy companions were a mismatch, and so thou did not receive wise counsel from them. Balto walked fast but Lyar walked slow, and you were caught in the middle, unsure whether to speed up or slow down.

"My child, if we can only walk as fast as those around us, thou must surround thyself with better people, successful people, the kind of people thou are proud of becoming. Before thou know it, thou will be walking not only at their speed, but at the pace thou desire.

"If thou want to remain where thou are right now, stay with thy companions of yesterday. But if thou seek to better thyself, seek friends who can truly help thou walk faster and leave the ones who hold thee back.

"My dear Shamash, thou are still young, and many roads still lay ahead of thee. Take thy time and despair not if thou cannot yet find that path set for thou. As thou meet new people, thou will discover that which thou truly desire. Soon, the road for thee will spread out like a paved path of stone and thou will no longer crawl at a snail's pace. With the right mindset and friends, thou may find thyself sprinting, and success in thy pursuit can be within thy reach.

"Now, go and find the friends of tomorrow who will push thou forward!"

STUDENT IN THE FOREST

Parable 22

AMONG MANY THINGS BABYLON VALUED, such as religion and military might, is knowledge. This was evident in the existence of temple schools across the city. Many of the teachers, who also worked as scribes, were strict and often punished underperforming students. This form of education, although arguable, helped Babylon become a technologically advanced and progressive civilization compared to its peers. This progress, as it so often does, slowly spreads to the villages around the great city.

However, one teacher, a scribe named Beltis, was less keen on the punishments and had a more practical approach to education. One that often required learning outside the halls of the temple school. For this reason, many students often sought advice from zir, especially on matters outside the school curriculum.

One particular afternoon in a village not far from the great walls, after the day's lectures were over, a student, Kadash, came up to Beltis. Kadash was among Beltis' best students. But that day, the seasoned scribe noticed their student looking reserved, with downcast eyes and a sullen look on their face.

"What happened, young Kadash?" Beltis asked. "You look as if one of your teachers struck the back of your hand with a cane."

Kadash chuckled, but their expression did not seem to be one of amusement. "No teacher was involved," Kadash said, "and no punishment was rendered upon me, either, oh wise Beltis."

"Then, pray tell, what can I help you with?"

Kadash hesitated for a moment, then breathed in and cleared their throat. "Why do parents do what they do, over and over again, even though doing so gives them or their child no benefit?"

"Are you, perhaps, speaking from your own experience?"

Kadash nodded. "It seems no detail can escape your discerning eyes, teacher, despite my efforts to be subtle about it."

"The expression on your face tells me this issue of yours is not a joyful one. If you are so concerned with your parent's repeated and unbeneficial behavior, this conduct may be happening often out of a bad habit. Am I correct?"

"It is as you say. My parent is addicted to drink. Our family may be well off and my parent does great work in trade, but everyday ze wastes most of zir coin on wine and beer and comes home drunk. Recently, however, ze caused trouble in our neighborhood, and I am afraid the situation will get worse if this continues."

Beltis pondered on their student's concern but thought it was too early to offer serious advice. "Have you confronted your parent about this?"

"I have not done so," Kadash answered, "for I fear ze might lash out or scold me."

"And when will you do so? When the sun rises in the west? When the Euphrates dries up and the floodplains harden? When the hallowed walls of Babylon turn back to dust?

"That is no good. I know not much of your parent's history, aside from what you told me, for me to offer you a solution. But speak to your parent for now. Voice out your concern. You will never solve anything if you keep your problems to yourself and do not take action. Should you wait until your family fortune runs out and you have nary a coin to spend for your learning and future? Waste not your time. Only after you have spoken to them and they still remain in their vice that you return to me."

Upon hearing these words, Kadash firmed their resolve and left the temple school.

A few days later, Kadash returned to the teacher. Kadash said their parent still had not stopped their vice despite Kadash telling them to cease this bad habit. The student became frustrated because of their parent's unchanging attitude.

"Why is my parent not listening to anything I say?" Kadash asked, their hands shaking and eyes on the verge of tears.

Beltis, hoping to ease the student's worries, smiled and said, "The power of habit is indeed a force to reckon. Let me explain it to you in a different way. Let us go for a walk."

The two walked a few blocks away from the school until they reached a secluded path that led to a small forest near the village. As they went down this road, Beltis turned to Kadash and said, "See that flower on the ground? Pull it up, stem and roots and all."

Kadash did as instructed and pulled up the flower with ease.

The pair continued walking, and then Beltis said, "Ah, look at that sapling at the side of the pathway ahead of us. Pull it up, just like what you did with the flower."

The student nodded and walked toward the sapling, grabbing it by its thin trunk and pulling it up. The young tree resisted a bit, so Kadash pulled a little harder and tore it from the ground with a small snapping sound. The student fell back on their backside, but got up and dusted themself. Ze held up the uprooted sapling in their hand like a warrior who just won a duel.

Again, they kept walking until they approached another sapling. This time, the small tree was about as tall as Beltis' chest. "Now, my dear student, pull up this tree."

Kadash paused and tilted their head. Ze wanted to question the teacher's instructions but thought twice about doing so and walked up to the young tree. The student looked at it from crown to root and puffed up their chest. Rubbing palms together, ze leaned down, grabbed the sapling's trunk close to the ground, pursed their lips, and pulled up.

The young tree was taller than the student, and its roots held tight to the soil underneath it. Twice Kadash tried to pull, and twice ze failed to remove the plant. Ze breathed in deep again and tried pulling the sapling side to side. Ze got on their knees, pulled again, and broke one, then two, of the roots. Kadash stood up again and, with all their might, pulled the sapling out of the ground. The rest of the roots snapped as their grip on the soil loosened and gave out.

Kadash let out a hearty sigh and laughed like how a soldier would after winning a battle. Beltis smiled and once more, the pair walked further down the road.

Near the end of the path, the teacher and student came across a great billowing tree. Its crown spread wide, covering most of its trunk, and on its leaves formed a thin crust of dust.

"I remembered seeing a similar plant adorning the Gardens of Semiramis," Kadash said.

"A tamarisk, perhaps," Beltis said, still beaming but with a subtle grin, "Now, young Kadash... please pull up this tree."

At this point, Kadash refused. "Teacher, this must be some sort of jest. This tree is fully grown, with a trunk so thick, branches of plenty, and roots running deep. If I am not careful, the dust on the leaves might get into my eyes. I can never pull it up from the ground, lest I strain my body and injure myself!"

"Nonsense," Beltis said. "If you truly desire to overcome this tree, you must rely not on your strength alone. Instead, gather the tools you need to cut it down. Spend long nights digging the soil around the roots. Break the branches off to pull it down easier. Take the tree apart, piece by piece if you have to, until you achieve your goal.

"However, pulling down this tree is not why we are here. Instead, ponder on this question: if the task is to simply pull out any tree, one can simply settle for a sapling rather than pull down this behemoth, can they not? If you let the tree grow for an age before pulling it out, this once simple task may turn into an all-consuming project.

"My wise student, what I mean to say is this: fixing bad habits is like pulling trees out of the ground. Stopping this habit early can help change one's behavior easily, just as how easily you pulled up the small sapling. But if you keep the bad habit alive year after year, its roots will go deeper and its trunk harder, just as a tree does. It will take a mighty force of will to pull it out by the roots to kill the habit.

"Yet, if you practice self-reflection, you will realize the bad habits holding you back in life. Then you can pull them out while they are still saplings, and you will have a much easier life. You need not wait for the roots to dig deep in your heart before taking action.

"What happened to your parent was that they let their bad habits take root over time. Now they, and even you, are struggling to pull them out.

"I can compare your situation to a foolish merchant who gambles away their hard-earned coin. At first, they gamble small amounts, for gambling at the onset is meant as a fun pastime. But as the vice grows and the merchant starts gambling and losing larger and larger sums, it gets harder to get the lost money back.

"Soon, they start borrowing from money lenders, but even that borrowed money is lost. See, if the merchant borrowed but a small amount, ze could easily pay it back. But as their loan gets bigger, it becomes difficult to pay all at once, like how pulling down a large tree becomes difficult for you.

"However, not all is lost. Just as a fully grown tree must be taken apart piece by piece to remove it from the ground, so must you and your parent take a gradual process to change that bad habit. Perhaps you can spend more time with your parent. Seek a priest or family friend who is proficient in handling these issues. Do not rush things. And maybe, given enough time, you will start seeing changes in your parent's behavior.

"Just as a bad habit can grow like a tree that is hard to pull down as time goes by, so can this habit be uprooted over time and with the proper tools."

THE POWERS OF BANKS

Parable 23

BEL THE EARTHENWARE PEDDLER scratched zir head while looking at the broken amphorae on the ground. Earlier, a crate of this fragile merchandise fell from zir cart when a panicking camel ran across the street and almost flipped the wooden ride.

"This misfortune appears to be the second time this month," Marduk, a textile merchant, told Bel while observing from a neighboring stall. "Are you certain you made your temple donations? Some gods can be quite fickle, especially when they feel ignored by mortals like us."

"Whether the gods were trying to teach me a lesson or I'm just down on my luck," Bel said, "losing plenty of quality wares means I am unlikely to profit today. Unless I can sell all my goods, that is. But that has never happened since I started this business of mine."

Marduk rubbed zir chin and gave Bel a thoughtful gaze. "When did you start this venture?"

"A little over two years ago. I used my parents' inheritance to start selling pottery. Until now, I only relied on my savings and profits to get by. But my inheritance was not a great sum, and so I never grew my business large enough to even afford a bonded servant to assist my enterprise. On profitable days, I can eat my fill. But on days like today, I may have to ration my bread to last until I can profit again."

"Such risks are part of our livelihood," Marduk said, "but I believe we need not degrade ourselves to living like beggars during unprofitable days. After all, a little self-respect should go a long way. Here's an idea: have you tried borrowing from a money lender?"

"My parents taught me to never borrow from others when I can afford to pay for something with my own money."

Marduk chuckled. "A sound advice, but also shortsighted. As a merchant, you should know this, even if you're fairly new."

"What do you mean?"

"Borrowing money to pay an expense is indeed unsavory, for doing so brings no potential to repay what you borrowed. But borrowing money to grow your business and increase profit... now that is something your parents might not have told you."

Bel paused and furrowed zir eyebrows. "I have not heard of this. How does borrowing grow my money further?"

Marduk smiled and placed a hand on Bel's shoulder. "First, let us clean up this broken merchandise of yours. Afterward, let me show you the power of banks and credit."

After helping Bel clear the street of the shattered amphorae, Marduk began the lesson.

"Suppose Fara is a prosperous person in the City of Atlantis, where the people's courts strictly regulate the banks, and the laws of the coins are as etched in stone as the sun rising in the east and the fire being hot. Fara is a money lender.

"It is not disputed that Fara has a great amount of coins, but most of it is tied to many projects. These coins labor all day and night for many cycles of the moon and are always growing. A prosperous farmer visited Fara not a fortnight ago to pay off zir loan in full. For this, the wise farmer bought a wide expanse of cheap dry desert land for a hefty sum of one hundred gold coins.

"This farmer, being a canal builder in zir youthful years, saw an opportunity to cut a small aqueduct as wide as one's hand. By mounding dirt at the bottom of the nearly flat property, this small trickle of water was able to flood the land in weeks. After several cycles of stopping the flow of life-giving water and letting the ground dry for several days, the wise farmer judged it was time to lay day seed for hay in the field and flood the land once again. With careful observation and management of the water, the farmer raised a scruffy but sizable crop the first season, then a respectable crop the second season. In the third season, ze was able to pay back Fara the one hundred gold coins, with interest, of course.

"Fara is very proud of this investment, because now there are a few families who do not pay the wise farmer a rent, as they live in tenements there and tend the crops in that land where before there was nothing but dust. Fara chuckles for this farmer does not grow grain as a crop, but ze grows gold coins as crops!"

"Is this what you mean by growing that which you borrowed?" Bel asked.

"Since you gain access to a larger sum of money by borrowing, you can use that amount for your business and purchase more goods to sell. Thus, your capacity to profit multiplies. Would you spend the ten gold coins you saved to purchase wares and sell them to gain five more? Imagine if you borrow a hundred."

The gears in Bel's mind started turning. "I can buy more earthenware to sell. In turn, I gain a higher profit."

"Putting it simply, yes." Marduk smiled. "However, there is more to borrowing than simply earning profit. Let us go back to my example.

"Fara, always looking to make coins work like servants, who, in turn, will make more servants over time, is seeking investment. That is when Ninti, a respectable baker apprentice in Babylon, approached Fara looking to acquire a loan to start zir own bakery in the city of Atlantis. More ambitious than the farmer, but hopefully just as wise, Ninti seeks a loan of one hundred gold coins, plus an all-important interest for Fara.

"Since Fara now has one hundred gold coins that ze wishes to put to work, Fara can make the hundred-gold coin loan to Ninti. In Atlantis, money lenders are allowed to lend out ten-to-one. In other words, for every real gold coin one has in the bank, it is allowed, by law, to lend out ten gold coins.

"The banks in Atlantis work on a system of credit, in which they can issue a low-value coin, often made of copper, which has the worth of one gold coin. This coin is called Atlantean Gold. This is a fiat currency, for the physical value of this coin is the value of the copper of which it is made. However, the government of the cities and the banks all know this coin has the value of gold despite being worth only copper.

"With Fara only having one hundred gold coins in the bank, ze can lend up to one thousand gold coins, like Atlantean Gold, payable back when the loan is paid in real gold coins.

"Now that Ninti has one hundred gold coins in Atlantean Gold fiat currency, ze can begin making a business. Ze buys an old building, paying a contractor to revitalize it to attract customers. The contractor also builds ovens of clay and brick to make the breads and great counters where Ninti puts the breads on display for customers to see. Ninti pays one hundred Atlantean Gold to the contractor, who is also a member of Fara's bank. Thus, Fara takes the one hundred coins from Ninti's account and places them in the contractor's account.

"Unfortunately, this venture is more expensive than Ninti believes it will be. For the building is found to be in extremely poor condition to improve. After several weeks of restoring it, the contractor notices the base of the walls have been slowly crumbling. So, after a meeting and running the numbers, Ninti finds the new cost of the bakery will be another 100 gold coins to rebuild the structure. This is not good news to Ninti, but ze must continue the project to pay off the original loan. So, Fara deposited another one hundred Atlantean Gold into the contractor's account.

"Such is the magic of credit. So, how much money does Fara truly have in the bank? One hundred gold coins. Even though the contractor has two hundred Atlantean Gold coins worth two hundred real gold coins in their bank account. This process can be repeated up to five more times until a ratio of ten-to-one is reached, even though Fara has no more than a hundred gold coins in the bank. This is the power of strong banking laws. They can allow businesses to grow on the belief of a positive future."

"In other words," Bel said, "borrowing also lets me cover circumstances unforeseen without having to rely solely on my profit?"

Marduk nodded. "Young peddler, you are beginning to see the beauty of credit. See, with your savings alone, you can only do so much. How will you replace those broken amphorae immediately if you have insufficient savings now? What if a customer wants to buy them from you today or tomorrow but you have not purchased a replacement? A lost opportunity can be avoided if you consider borrowing, especially when demand for your wares is high and you are confident you can sell them quickly.

"In a society without credit, the only way to start a venture is to save money for this enterprise. And if unforeseen roadblocks occur, they may stop the progress of growth altogether.

"It is known far and wide that Atlantis is a prosperous city, even though banks are allowed to lend out ten gold coins for every real gold coin in their possession. This also means if all the account holders in Fara's bank suddenly demand their money back, Fara's bank will quickly collapse unless the Great Ruler of the City steps in to save it. Sounds like an elaborate fraud , does it not? But if it is, the entire economy is a fraud. But if everyone has faith in the system, it can make great progress at a rapid pace.

"The fact is it's not a deception, but rather a tribute to the amazing abilities of the human imagination. That is what enables banks and the entire economy to survive. And flourish is our trust in the future. This trust is the soul backing most of the money in the city.

"Fara is placing the money in the contractor's account trusting that one day, the bakery will be profitable and able to pay back the Atlantean Gold, over time, with real gold coins, even though the bakery has not baked a single sweet cake yet. If you think about it, how else can an entrepreneur start a new business without having the coin in hand? It is hard to find a contractor who will work without coins today, in hopes of coins in the future.

"The entire enterprise is thus founded on trust in an imaginary future. The trust that the entrepreneur and the money lender have in the bakery of their dreams, along with the contractor's trust in the future solvency of the bank.

"This is why credit allows economies to grow at a great pace." Marduk paused and smiled at Bel. "Thus, young peddler, I hope you can decide soon whether to remain in your parents' way of doing business or open up to the world of credit and see the potential of your enterprise for growth. The choice is yours."

THE POWER OF LAW

Parable 24

THE COURTYARD OF NARAMSIN'S HOUSE doubled as a place for merchants to sell their wares. Due to this residence's location near Babylon's commercial district, a few enterprising people preferred to do business here. As such, Naramsin reserved one corner of that cool, airy courtyard for Daon, a young upstart money lender. This way, should any merchant be in need of a quick coin, access to it would be convenient.

As Naramsin went downstairs to the courtyard one fine afternoon, ze noticed Daon sitting slouched and head down in the corner. The middle-aged lord of the house headed toward the money lender's stall.

"May the God of Good Luck bless us today," a beaming Naramsin greeted. "Alas, thou appear to have eaten a bad lunch. Are thou in need of an asu to deal with thy illness?"

"Your usual greeting should have comforted me if I received it in the morning," Daon said, wincing. "And no, I am not sick and definitely not in need of strong drink or any other doctor. I am simply dealing with a troublesome client."

"Ah, let me guess. Merodach the saddle maker?"

"So, you've heard?" Daon said, with wide eyes looking up to Naramsin. "Zir payment was two weeks due. Yet even with Merodach's promises and the extended time I gave, not once has ze showed up in your humble abode, and now it appears ze has gone missing!"

Naramsin chuckled. "Young Daon, I have seen many a money

lender in such a situation as thee. Some of them have been working in this business far longer than thou. Yet they still committed mistakes, a few of them not once but several times."

Daon shook zir head. "Mistakes?"

"Thou are still young and maybe a little impulsive. I understand why thou lent thirty gold coins to Merodach. After all, that is a hefty sum, and, had ze stayed true to zir commitment to pay thee back with interest, thou should be feasting now than sulking in this dark corner."

"So, what mistake did I commit?"

"Did thou even bother uncovering Merodach's circumstances before lending to them? A wise money lender should be able to discern a good investment from a bad one. Merodach had for the past few months been gambling carelessly to the point where ze had to dip into their business just to fund zir vice. Did thou even know this?"

"I..." Daon paused. "Merodach spoke so convincingly, and I got swept by such silver tongue. And in my greed after hearing their promise of paying back more than the principal and interest, we shook hands and I did not bother asking any further."

Naramsin chuckled again. "Tell me, will Merodach's nonpayment drive thee down the street and turn thee into a beggar? There are other more trustworthy clients, and I believe as long as thy business prospers, thou shall continue to have food on the table and a roof over thy head. But if thou is serious about getting thy money back, does this great city of Babylon give thee the means to do so?"

Daon looked up at the sky and mused. "Did the Great Ruler of the City not enact laws regarding loans and interest?"

"Indeed," Naramsin replied with a smile. "If thou cannot trust the person, why not trust the laws and financial systems of the city where thou do business? After all, these laws are what made Babylon prosperous. Here, let me tell thee a story.

"How exactly did Atlantis become the wealthiest city in the world, with only Babylon being able to compare? By having its people put their trust in the law and in the financial system. They were adamant about paying their dues on time, with standard punishments for those who did not. The city was fond of extending credit to promising enterprises through registered companies rather than individuals. This way, should the God of Good Luck not shine on them, the law will have their backs.

"Their government has, separate from the Great Ruler of the City, a judicial system that puts a high value on the protection of private rights.

"It has happened many times before and will happen many more times in the future. The shrewd investor will seek to store their wealth in places that emphasize protecting their private property, and away from unfair cities, and put a higher importance on the Great Ruler of the Cities' every wish. This is why many wise investors have made the long trek to Atlantis.

"Imagine thou is the descendant of an Egyptian family in good standing. Thou have taken thy education and tried thy hand at several jobs. Thy wise parent now wishes for thee to go to other cities and expand the family business passed down through generations. So, they send thee to Atlantis and thy sibling of the same age to Waset, a month's caravan ride south of Egypt along the Nile.

"You are each given one hundred gold coins to invest.

"Thy sibling lends their capital to the Pharaoh of Waset, who needs this coin to fight the desert tribes controlling the southern stretch of the Nile.

"Meanwhile, thou goes to Atlantis to invest it in a new road built by private citizens to charge a toll for each traveler. Suppose the road is an immense success because people now travel much quicker on it than on the common dirt paths of the time. Especially the caravans, with their heavy wagons that would otherwise be prone to being stuck in the mud. The tolls are adding up nicely. So nicely, in fact, the city council wishes to buy the rights to the road so they can raise and lower the tolls as they please. Thou do agree and they pay off thy loan with interest. Afterward, thou sends word to thy wise parent and they reply they are pleased.

"But thy sibling is becoming nervous. While the war with the tribes on the riverbanks is proving to be successful and the city has conquered new territory, a new band of rebels, unknown to the city before, begins attacking the new lands. The pharaoh, too prideful to lose these lands, promises the citizens of Waset new farmlands and asks for every copper ze can get their hands on, even if this means foregoing paying old debts.

"Thy sibling is worried about getting their principal back and sends messages to the palace asking the pharaoh's court to intercede but to no success. Thus, not only has thy sibling not gained the much-desired interest on the loan, but the principal is now lost as well. Thy parent is not pleased with thy sibling.

"To add more anxiety to a stressful situation, the pharaoh sends an official to thy sibling's dwelling and says, in clear terms, that they expect to receive another loan of the same size, sooner than later.

"Thy sibling, being out of capital, writes to thy good parent once again and persuades them that the pharaoh will honor their debts once the second loan is given and the tribes are defeated. The parent, who has always been known to be an optimist, decides to trust in the wisdom of their child who lives in a faraway city and sends another one hundred gold coins—which is promptly consumed by the provisioning of great rowed ships of war to be sent up the Nile. Thy sibling is most anxious at the start of this new investment, because ze saw the scribe record the loan on a clay tablet but did not give thy sibling a copy as a receipt. Ze was simply escorted out of the palace after lending the money.

"During this tumultuous period for thy sibling, things are looking bright for thee in Atlantis. Thou has made more loans with enterprising Atlantis businesspeople who have consistently returned thy principal and interest within the agreed time frame.

"But as all good things eventually come to an end, thou makes an unwise loan. Thou invested in two hundred heads of cattle, purchased from a trader by the person who has arranged the loan before seeing the animals themselves. With food in short supply in Atlantis due to several storms over the past week, thou believes this herd of cattle will make a quick profit in the market. But as the herd approaches the city road, a soldier informs the broker these animals have red spots with black dots in the middle. Everyone knows cattle with these infectious spots must be led away from the city and killed at least 100 paves away from water, lest they infect other cattle or cause the children to get sick.

"The merchant who has brokered the loan now refuses to pay back this loan on the cattle, causing thee to lose thy principal.

"When thou writes to thy good parent to inform them of this, they are furious and demand both thee and thy sibling hire lawyers to settle these outstanding debts. Thus, thou does file a complaint in Atlantis at the Merchant Justice Building while thy sibling files suit against the pharaoh.

"What makes the justice system of Atlantis unique is its

separation from the influences of the crown and the great mobs of the street. In thy situation, the honorable person who reviews this case decides that the contract written on thin wood and recorded in the hall of public records is legitimate and does state that the borrower must pay back the lender if the lender buys diseased cattle that must be put down.

"So, with due process, the court delivers a verdict in favor of thee, the lender, and sends court deputies to the borrower's domicile to make them pay up or sell zir property to repay zir due debt.

"Meanwhile, in Waset, the judges, appointed by the pharaoh, hold lucrative positions but understand the consequences of ruling against their patron and are thus often driven to act in fear. These judges dismiss the suit and have thy sibling arrested for the made-up charge of disturbing the peace. Authorities put them in a cell for two days without food or water as punishment.

"Viewing from the outside, thy wise parent can see the difference in their offsprings' situations and has learned their lesson in dealing with pharaohs and the Great Ruler of Cities. For thy parent, trusting in a justice system that does not waver from the laws is better than trying to extract even a bent copper from a pharaoh.

"The story gets worse for thy poor sibling, though. The Pharaoh of Waset, ignorant of shipbuilding, has made desert people build the boats of war to be sent through the Nile instead of the more expensive boat builders in Egypt who can build mighty galleys that can survive the salt waters and rough waves of the sea. So, the war boats, having been built at great cost to defeat the tribes up the river, sank quickly after meeting the enemy.

"With their navy gone, the pharaoh is now in their greatest need yet of coin to protect the now disputed riverlands. So, ze has the judges issue trumped-up charges against thy sibling for conspiracy and puts them in jail. They then demand a ransom of one thousand gold coins for thy sibling's release, or ze shall be tortured to death.

"Naturally, thy parent is at their wit's end. Although ze pays the ransom for thy sibling's release, thy parent now refuses to do any more business with any pharaoh. Instead, thy parent decides to move their family and cousins to Atlantis, where they can prosper honestly. Knowing how that city has dealt with thy ordeal, thy parent is confident thy family and relatives will have no prospect of being imprisoned for failure to give thy hard-earned coin to unworthy borrowers.

"This is why Atlantis has grown so wealthy, because of its just laws. People from other cities have learned the hard way that the whims of rulers cost everyone their hard-earned coin. So, it is always wise to do business in places with strong protections and strict laws. These laws are why Babylon is so safe; one can walk the street on a night without a moon. I believe people will be talking about these laws for thousands of years to come."

With this narration from Naramsin, Daon regained some sense of relief and managed to breathe easier. Ze thanked the lord of the house and, on the next day, Daon headed to the authorities responsible for enforcing Babylon's laws and upholding the city's financial systems. Meanwhile, Naramsin continued to greet the merchants in their courtyard in the same cheerful manner as ze did with Daon.

THE MIND'S GARDEN

Parable 25

ON A VAST COUNTRYSIDE across the western bank of the Euphrates, on the outskirts of Babylon, stood the landowner Haban. As the sun was about to set, ze tolled a bell to signal the farmers to cease their toil on zir farm. The workers let out a modest cheer for their well-deserved rest after a long day.

"Hear ye, all who have labored since the start of this summer season," Haban announced. "The barley harvest is upon us. By my reckoning, the grains should give us a promising yield, more than they did in previous harvests. As a thanksgiving to the gods, let us hold a humble celebration tonight."

With these words, the farmers and their families prepared their contributions for a shared meal and entertainment over a bonfire for that night.

In the midst of the preparations, one of the workers, a young freeperson named Aralu, approached Haban. Aralu had in hand a small pouch that clinked and jingled with a sound Haban recognized.

"Something appears to trouble thy mind, young Aralu," Haban said with a deep, soft voice that had a hint of pleasantry. "Is that thy savings from laboring on this land for which I hired thee? No, the pouch seems heavier and of a different quality than what thou do typically tie to thy belt."

"It is indeed different, as what you have said," Aralu said. "Last month, while your crops were not yet ready for harvesting, I took a week off since I had no essential work to do at that time. I went to the walled city of Babylon when I chanced upon a certain landowner. Over beers and cheese, ze shared stories and talked about zir need for farm workers. Ze also observed me from head to toe and figured I was a farmhand. We became friends that day.

"A week ago, I saw the landowner again. This time, ze offered me work tending to their farmland south of here. Fruits like dates and pomegranates and vegetables like onions, lentils, leeks, and much more are their produce. From that variety, it appears to guarantee employment all year round."

With both hands, Aralu held the pouch in front of Haban's face.

"This," Aralu said, "is an advanced payment I received from them, one-tenth of what I can earn should I decide to relocate to that region."

Haban narrowed zir eyes and smiled, the wrinkles of age forming around zir cheeks. "Thou are a freeperson, young Aralu. I hired thee for thou had in thy eyes a passion to bring forth a barley harvest unlike what this land ever had, and the past seasons proved to be so. Unlike a bonded servant with no such will to choose, thou have free reign over thy choices.

"Thus, if thou do feel it is in thy favor to seek a better life and security in other places, I am in no position to hold thee back. In fact, even if thou no longer work for me, I believe this land shall continue to prosper."

"Your intuition amazes me, Elder Haban," Aralu said with a nod. "I wish not to boast of my work on your land. But I am in awe of your optimism that you will keep producing better crops one season after another even when workers, especially freepersons like me, come and go."

Haban laughed. "Thou do sound as if I will lose a great asset should I not stop thee from leaving.

"But thou are right, except for one small thing: when determining my loss, not only do I consider freepeople under my hire who leave, but bonded servants, too. Thou sees, when these servants get sick or disabled or, gods forbid, get stolen from me or disappear, can they do work on my field as much as the healthy ones can? No? In that case, bonded servants are no different from freepeople who leave and seek better pay from other employers. I must, therefore, be prepared for such eventualities.

"Besides, if I wallow too much on my losses, I may become doubtful of prosperous days, too. Remember the famine that occurred not long ago? Not only did it devastate my land and produce, but the war that followed soon after brought further destruction as well. For years, my property produced nothing, even after the famine and war were over. Then I saw my neighbors down south producing bountiful harvests. Any other farmer in my situation would become jealous.

"But rather than give up, I used the savings I kept in a safe place within the great walls of Babylon and even borrowed coin from money lenders so I could revitalize my farm. And now, the fruits of my labor, with the help from my bonded servants and hired freepersons like thee, has led to this rich harvest.

"What I mean to say is, while preparation helps thee overcome unforeseen circumstances, so does being in a proper state of mind."

"Preparation, I can understand," Aralu said. "But one's state of mind? How so?"

Haban led Aralu to sit on a reed mat on the ground nearby.

Before Haban began, a few workers lit some tinder to start the bonfire. Haban then continued, "All you are today and all thou will ever be is based on thy mind.

"From successful people to total losers, they all live lives based on the framework of their minds.

"In school, we are taught numbers, letters, and facts. We are not taught that how we think and the actions we take based on those thoughts will forever guide our life.

"For example, thou would not expect an athletic person to think of exercise without a positive intent.

"When people talk about success, they usually talk about the accumulation of money. This is because humans are naturally petty and jealous beings. We cannot be trusted to cooperate without fixed units of value for fair trade. Thus, we need money to run a society. And thus, accumulating money gives a person a powerful thing… choice. With choice, we have the ability to live the life we desire, not the life we got sucked into to survive.

"Our mind is like a garden. For children, it is bare dirt. With learning and new experiences, we fertilize this dirt, and plants begin to appear. Simple plants at first, such as grasses and mosses. Then, more diverse and complex ones, such as flowers and zucchini, start to appear. Like a garden, a mind naturally goes wild without added effort to keep it pure. Weeds begin to grow, bugs eat the roots, and the plants appear disheveled by not being properly tended.

"We leave school with a garden that has a few intricate plants, such as tulips, and hardy plants, like potatoes, to sustain us. But we pay no mind to the small weeds sprouting. Then as we gain independence past our teenage years, without proper vigilance, our gardens grow wild. If this goes on for too long, the dirt will be exhausted of nutrients, and nothing but the humble grasses will grow there.

"And when we think our carelessness is not enough, we see our neighbors' gardens with the towering fruit trees, and we turn jealous and spiteful.

"This is where the power of the mind comes into play. No one can mind our garden but ourselves. We cannot fault our neighbor for having their fields yield a better harvest. Thus, we must tend to our own, for that is what we have control of."

After speaking these words, Haban saw Aralu's face lighten like the bonfire that began blazing with warmth.

"If thou wishes still to seek work in other places," Haban said, "I give thee my blessing, as long as thou keep my words in thy heart."

"I will," Aralu replied. "After this barley harvest, I shall give you my decision."

Haban beamed. "Remember to keep thy mind healthy and organized to fend off weeds. So that the simple vegetables thou has planted in thy mind's garden now may lead to tulips, to roses, to fruit trees, and even to the towering timbers of the north."

WILL POWER IS LIKE A MUSCLE

Parable 26

OLD BABYLON AT ITS HEIGHT had great structures of palaces, temples, and gardens surrounded by strong, massive walls that had turned many an invader away. And more than its sprawling architectural marvels, this ancient metropolis had citizens accomplished in the ways of education, law, and religion.

However, one other facet of Babylonians not extensively explored was how they kept their bodies and minds healthy.

Ancient Babylonians often participated in sports, such as wrestling and boxing, and might have enjoyed other games like polo. After all, Gilgamesh, a prominent figure in their mythology, was said to have taken part in these activities that tested one's physical prowess.

Because these sports entail plenty of physical movement, one could expect participants to exercise and build up their bodies to be healthy and strong. And when the body and its muscles were conditioned for these games, the gods might bless the athlete with the gift of victory.

Palassar the Amorite was no stranger to these physical activities, for sports were common among soldiers. As a seasoned member of Babylon's household troops, it was expected of zir to maintain a high degree of physical competence, often demonstrated through these sports, not only to fight enemies but ensure the Great Ruler of the City's safety.

As Palassar stood guard at one of Babylon's palaces one evening, amid the flames and warmth of a nearby firepit, a new recruit by the name of Ashkabal approached zir and saluted.

"Thou must be my replacement," Palassar said. "The bell for the changing of the guard had long since rung, and yet thou took a while to arrive here."

"My apologies," Ashkabal said, panting. "As I am but a new recruit, I am yet to get used to this task of keeping time and guarding the palace."

Palassar grunted. "Such an excuse might be acceptable for a regular soldier, but not for the royal household troops. We guard not only the palaces against intruders but also the security of the Great Ruler of the City. What will happen should an assassin enter our ruler's bed chambers on thy watch simply because thou were not at thy post at the appointed time?"

Ashkabal had no words and kept zir head low. Palassar sighed and observed from head to foot the soldier illuminated by the firepit's flames. Ashkabal, a young citizen who recently turned into an adult, had a toned but lanky body underneath their armor. Palassar shook zir head.

"Soldier," Palassar said, "canst thou run ten leagues and back in thy full battle gear? A soldier from among the freepeople can do so, but the royal household troops do twice, even thrice, that distance."

"Wise Palassar," Ashkabal addressed, "as I am now, I can do as well as a freeperson serving the army, but not enough to run the distance expected of a soldier of our esteemed force. And yet, my parent, one of high standing in the palace, had appointed me part of this honored outfit despite my scrawny build and unremarkable skill with a sword and spear.

"See here, my arms are weak, my thighs frail, and my knees shaky. When I hold a sword or spear for too long, the skin on my palms breaks. When I hold a shield, it looks like the shield is holding me instead.

"But your arms, they are like hammers, and your thighs look as strong as a bull's. When I stand beside you, I feel like a prey about to be devoured by a predator. At times, I would feel demotivated and think my parents made a mistake for putting me here.

"And yet, I am here, a mismatch to the rest of this force. Still, I cannot bring dishonor, for my performance will reflect not only on my family but on the Great Ruler's army and, thus, to the Great Ruler." Ashkabal paused. "Tell me, oh wise Palassar, what must I do to be a soldier worthy of the royal household troops?"

Understanding Ashkabal's circumstance, Palassar could not bring zirself to punish the young recruit for tardiness. But Palassar felt ze could not leave zir post without at least imparting wisdom to this green soldier.

"Listen, and listen well, young Ashkabal," Palassar said, feeling in zir chest a growing fire, almost as strong as the cackling flames in the firepit. "Every day, we train. Sunrise, midday, and sunset, we train. At times of peace, we train. During war, we train. Doing so helps strengthen thy body and makes thou skilled with thy weapons and fists. So, when the enemy comes and shakes our swords, spears, and shields, we have a better likelihood of survival and victory.

"Now, starting is the hard part. In thy mind, thou will grumble and complain, and thy muscles will get sore. But thou has to keep at it. Soon, thou will get used to the routine and it gets easier. The weapons thou do carry that once were heavy will be light, and the spear thou do throw no farther than a few feet will fly farther. But thou still must train every day."

Palassar could see Ashkabal shake and become pale after that monologue. Sweat formed on the young soldier's forehead, and Palassar knew this adolescent child had a long way to go.

Then, like the firepit's flames shifting direction as the wind blew the opposite way, Ashkabal's expression changed. Ze pursed zir lips, curled the skin between zir eyebrows, and tightened zir fists.

"Then, wise Palassar," Ashkabal began, with eyes reflecting the bright flames, "what must I do to overcome this unmotivated, passive attitude of mine and become strong?"

Palassar smiled. "Willpower," ze said. "Thou might think it's rare to encounter an established routine that trains us to just do what we need to do. But willpower is like thy muscles. Just as training and exercise help build and strengthen thy body, so too can they help increase thy willpower. And when thou has developed thy willpower, apply it to activities that enhance thy life. Willpower can help thee get through that difficult start of physical training and maintain discipline in thy day-to-day."

Ashkabal nodded in response, but the stiff movement of zir head made Palassar think there was still some hesitance on the young recruit's part.

Then, Ashkabal asked, "The physical training… I have some idea of it. Plenty of times have I seen soldiers drill together. Though many, they move as one. And so, I only need to follow the sergeant or other officer to know what exercise to perform and move in unison with the others. Rather, what I need to know… is how to develop my willpower."

"If that is thy desire," the seasoned warrior said, "then, my young soldier, I shall tell of two ways in which thou can improve thy willpower. Let us begin with the first one, which involves training thy mind and body in a highly intensive manner.

"See, willpower is something we all have in abundance at times, but often not when we need it most. Has thou ever woken up in the morning, before the sun rose, to do thy duty, only to stay up late without rest? What about setting up camp and pitching tents during a war campaign? These extraordinary days require much more energy than usual. And often, the willpower thou has in the beginning will not last that long.

"Now, thou may have great strength and peerless skill in battle. But without willpower, thou are no more useful than a wounded soldier in a field hospital.

"If thou wish to improve thy life and prowess as a soldier, thou must train to improve thy willpower. One way to do so is performing highly intensive but beneficial activities, such as doing pushups to build up thy upper body strength or running ten leagues and back carrying full battle gear to improve endurance."

Ashkabal rubbed zir chin. "I can perform pushups fairly well. Running ten leagues and back, well... perhaps with enough willpower..."

Palassar laughed. "Suppose thou do start these exercises with enthusiasm. Thou might do fifty pushups on thy first attempt and perhaps cover twenty leagues in a day. What will thou feel after doing them?"

"I must admit, those numbers are too high for me. But if by some blessing of the gods or force of will that I could, I might feel too sore to continue afterward, and I might collapse from fatigue."

"See, thy mind may think thou canst do things thy body has not been trained to do. And so, thou do overdo them, and thy body ends up getting too sore. Thy enthusiasm not restrained will spill out like a boiling, overflowing cauldron, and thou might end up getting burned.

"Can thou train thy willpower this way? Possibly, and some people have succeeded in doing so. But the highly intensive nature of this method can exhaust thee to the point of soreness. If thou do continue doing so, with careless thought and without restraint, thou might end up harming thyself more."

"If that is so," Ashkabal spoke up, "how should I train my body and willpower so I do not end up hurting myself?"

"First, know thy limits, and start off in a slow but consistent manner. This is the second way of improving thy willpower. Rather than pushing beyond thy limits on the first attempt, keep thy exercises within a manageable pace. Do so and thou may achieve highly efficient results.

"Perhaps thou do want to achieve fifty pushups or cover twenty leagues in a day. Start slow, be consistent, and build on thy success. Each day for a week, do ten pushups or run for ten minutes regardless of the distance covered. After each week, increase thy daily exercise by an additional ten pushups or ten minutes of running. Through this method, thou can increase thy willpower and strengthen thy body as well. Consistency is crucial."

"I understand," Ashkabal said, nodding. "Still, I am prone to getting distracted and demotivated, and I am afraid I might eventually slow down or stop without achieving my goal."

Palassar reminisced about the times other soldiers spoke of that to him. "Thou are not the first soldier who confessed to me such shortcomings. After all, humans have evolved in environments where conserving energy is essential. When we constantly fail at a task, do we not get discouraged and prefer more pleasurable activities? Laziness is natural and is why we began farming thousands of years ago.

"And yet, laziness that does not breed innovation can be detrimental. So, if thou want to overcome this behavior, start slow and build consistency, allowing thy subconscious to see the task as manageable. Do so and thy daily ritual of ten pushups or ten minutes of running will have eventually increased before thee realize it. If thou do keep at it for a month or two, thou might see thyself doing fifty pushups or even running twenty leagues as naturally as breathing.

"Thou can also introduce new routines to thy exercise to break the monotony. Perhaps some soldiers in our esteemed unit will challenge thee to a friendly match of boxing or wrestling. Winning can be a powerful motivation and may even help build up thy willpower."

Palassar once more saw the firepit's flames reflecting in Ashkabal's eyes, but brighter this time.

"I feel your words are giving me strength," Ashkabal said, the quiver in zir voice dissipating and the tremble in zir knees gone. "I know my body is less capable than yours. But despite your words, my mind is now telling me I can do more than ten pushups today!"

Laughter erupted from Palassar's mouth once again. "See what I meant about enthusiasm? The amount of workout thou can do in a day varies. However, thou cannot keep adding more pushups indefinitely, for the human body has a limit. Find thy balance, such as one and a half hours of productivity in the morning and another half-hour in the evening.

"Say, thou dedicate thirty minutes each day for exercise and productivity for sixty and two hundred days of work in a year. Thou wilt have thirty and one hundred hours of productivity annually. Perhaps that will be thy balance. Then, as thy muscles and willpower improve over the months and years, that balance may change. But that discussion will be for another time.

“Remember, Babylon’s walls, temples, and palaces were not built in a day, and this city’s greatness did not occur overnight. But the small yet consistent daily actions thou do will lead to extraordinary results. Start slow, be consistent, and watch thy willpower grow. With each step, thou are not only building a habit, thou are building a future. Embrace the journey, and let thy willpower transform thy life.

“The path to success is within thy reach, as long as thou do thy tasks one step, one day at a time. Keep pushing forward, and soon, thou wilt look back and be amazed at how far thou has come.”

CHIPPING OF STONE

Parable 27

ON THE OUTSKIRTS OF BABYLON lived Amurum, a potter with a fair success in their trade. Aside from crafting mud bricks, ceramic bowls, and colored tiles, Amurum also created figures of clay. Many satisfied clients bought their products not only for the quality but the reasonable price.

One hot afternoon, as Amurum was out in the courtyard of their workshop inspecting a batch of bricks being dried, a trader named Hassimir arrived bringing several crates of clay.

"My good friend Hassimir," Amurum greeted, their face still caked with dried flakes of mud from their labor this morning, "You are late! Were you not supposed to arrive yesterday?"

"One of my carts became stuck in the floodplains," Hassimir said, shaking their head. "It was so heavy it almost sank in the mud. Took almost half a morning to pull it out."

Amurum looked at the crates behind Hassimir. "If so, the quality of your clay should be worth your troubles, then."

Hassimir huffed and grinned. "For the past three years I traded with you, was there a time I sold you clay of less quality than you required? None, I say! In turn, you have produced wares of superior quality that even scribes and rich people praise. This time is no different. Better, even!"

"Quite the salesperson you are," Amurum said, chuckling. "But enough flattery. I have another delivery for you. This time, it is for that one client of mine who you met last week. Come, I will show you the products."

The two headed toward the storage room near the courtyard. Once they were inside, Amurum opened the crate to be delivered and showed Hassimir the wares.

"Clay dolls?" Hassimir asked. "For a religious purpose, I assume. Perhaps to be placed on an altar?"

"Indeed. I trust you can deliver them with utmost care."

Hassimir stayed silent for a moment, their eyes sparkling as ze stared at the figures. They had intricate detail and were sculpted and painted in such a fashion that the trader thought they would move like a golem at any moment.

"Such fine creations you have here," Hassimir said, almost whispering, as if wary of saying a magic spell by accident and turning the figures into living beings. "The clay dolls you created long ago would pale in comparison to these precious things."

"Again, you flatter too much," Amurum said. "You will not receive more coin from me than what we agreed upon, if that is what you are after."

"Oh, no, no, my friend," Hassimir stuttered, waving their hand. "I simply want to ask how you improved your craft and produced these dolls that seem about to… jump out of the crate and run away, if one were not careful."

Amurum chuckled. "In that case, let me tell you a tale, if you are not so pressed for time.

"Long ago, there was a person who inherited a piece of land from a distant relative. On this land, a giant boulder loomed, almost as tall as a person. From the moment ze saw that boulder, the landowner disliked it from the bottom of their heart. The rock appeared like a tumor on what could have been a healthy piece of property. An ugly, stubborn obstacle in the middle of an otherwise promising landscape.

"For weeks, ze brooded over how to get rid of this boulder. Ze considered every possible method, such as hiring workers to hammer the stubborn protuberance apart. But each idea proved either too expensive or too difficult. However, as time passed and the longer the boulder remained, something within the landowner began to change.

"Perhaps, ze thought, this stubborn rock could be more than just a problem. What if, instead of fighting it, ze could transform it into something beautiful? Something that could make this misplaced hunk of hardened earth fit in the scenery?

"And so, with newfound resolve, the landowner picked up a chisel and began to work, slowly chipping away at the stone. Day by day, the boulder that had once caused so much frustration began to take on a new shape, revealing a potential that had been hidden from the start. The person realized the boulder was no longer just a rock but a symbol of patience, creativity, and power to turn challenges into opportunities.

"The landowner knew this transformation would not happen overnight. Such a task required time, patience, and unwavering dedication. Each evening, after the day's duties were done, ze would gather the proper tools and set to work, chipping away bit by bit. Ze understood that by working on the rock for even only two hours a day and at a constant pace, zir efforts would amount to a full thirty days of work by year's end. With this in mind, ze approached the boulder with steady commitment, never rushing the process, knowing that true change would take time.

"As weeks turned into months and months into years, the villagers began to notice the landowner's efforts. Occasionally, a neighbor would pass by, curious about the progress. They would find the landowner, calm and focused, working with methodical precision. Some offered words of encouragement, while others wondered in silence if all this effort would amount to anything more than a pile of rubble.

“But the landowner remained untroubled by others’ opinions and understood that meaningful change did not come all at once. Rather, it was the result of persistent effort—small, steady steps that, over time, led to something extraordinary. The landowner was not just carving away at the boulder; ze was practicing a way of life, turning frustration into a path of growth.

“By the end of the second year, the landowner decided it was time to share the fruits of labor. Ze sent out invitations and welcomed the community for a special unveiling. The villagers arrived at the house, eager to see what had become of the boulder on the land. As they approached, they were met with an astonishing sight.

“The boulder, once an unflattering piece of rock, had been transformed into a magnificent sculpture of a horse, captured mid-stride, with every detail rendered with exquisite care as if it might gallop away at any moment.

“The crowd was in awe, their whispers of admiration growing as they marveled at the seemingly realistic beauty before them. The intricate and masterful carvings on the stone made some onlookers wonder whether it was a real horse petrified by some form of magic.

“Finally, someone in the crowd asked the question on everyone’s mind, ‘Oh wise and ingenious fellow, how did you do this? How did an ordinary rock that once stained the eyes and blighted the land turn into such a masterpiece?’

“The landowner smiled and replied, ‘I simply chipped away

everything that wasn't a horse.'

"A few villagers who understood the wit laughed at the answer. Others, not wanting to appear ignorant, nodded in agreement, though they were baffled by the response. What did it mean to chip away everything that was not a horse? How could such a simple, playful statement explain the extraordinary transformation?

"As the villagers murmured among themselves, with some still wondering what the landowner meant, a young person named Mylitta emerged from the crowd. Known for their inquisitive nature and fearlessness to seek clarity, Mylitta approached the landowner and asked, 'Wise sculptor, how can I become like you, someone who can turn an ugly rock into something beautiful?'

"With soft eyes and a subtle smile, the landowner looked at Mylitta and said, 'My young friend, in the same way I transformed this boulder, you must look within yourself and chip away everything that is not great. It may sound simple, but it is far from easy. Each of us is like a great stone boulder —stubborn and resistant to change. But with patience and determination, we can shape ourselves into something better, something new.'

"The landowner continued, 'Too often, we let our emotions stray us like dogs chasing their next meal, reacting to life rather than shaping it. But we can choose instead to live like the beaver that diligently builds a dam to create a home or the humble spider that spins a web to catch tomorrow's meal. These creatures teach us the value of foresight and persistence.'

"Mylitta listened closely as the landowner spoke. 'To become wise,' the landowner continued, 'to create beauty from what seems ordinary, you must first envision the life you want to lead. Then, begin the work of chipping away from your present life everything that does not belong to that vision.

" 'You need not rush into things. If you do, you might make mistakes. You might chip off more stone than you would have wanted or break the leg or tail of your sculpture. It is not about making drastic changes overnight, but about taking small, consistent steps every day.'

"The landowner paused, letting the words sink into the young person's head before continuing. 'Remember, Mylitta, transformation is a gradual process. Just as it took me years to shape this boulder into a horse, you will also take time to shape yourself into the person you wish to be. If you are patient and persistent, you will find that the life you create is as beautiful and unique as this sculpture.'

"With a renewed sense of purpose, Mylitta left with the knowledge that their journey ahead would be challenging, but ze was determined to follow the wise landowner's advice. As ze walked back through the village, Mylitta felt a spark of excitement in the heart—a spark that would one day ignite the flame of transformation.

"The villagers, too, left the landowner's house with much to ponder. The landowner's words resonated with them in unexpected ways. Over time, they would realize the lesson of the boulder and the horse was not just about creating art, but about the power of persistence, vision, and the quiet, steady work of self-improvement."

"A quite enlightening tale you have told me," Hassimir said. "As a trader who only makes money harvesting clay and selling wares but never creating or crafting anything new, I have never understood your craft. Now I realize why you can make beautiful clay figures today compared to when I first traded with you. The patience and persistence it must have taken you to come to this point... I see why many clients are willing to pay good money to get hold of your products."

"The effort is not mine alone," Amurum rebutted. "The clay you bring me may appear ordinary to some people. Troublesome even, as it can cause carts and animals to get stuck and be unable to move. But in the hands of a skilled artisan, its value can become worth more than you can imagine.

"Furthermore, learning to carve yourself into a better person, chipping away the things that do not make you, can help increase your value. The skills and personality we hone in life, slowly but persistently, can help us become even more precious than that stone horse sculpture or these clay dolls."

A FISHER OF THE NILE

Parable 28

A WISE PERSON NAMED SUMSHIR was walking along the great River Nile one morning. Ze was part of a caravan, headed from Babylon to Egypt, that set up camp by the riverside. The camels needed resting, and Sumshir, not being the spry child of earlier days who raced with camels on foot for fun, thought spending a night or so near the river would be a nice respite.

As ze walked barefoot along the shore, wading their feet on the cold, soothing water lapping the sand, Sumshir recalled the time ze heard traveling merchants talk about Egypt's grand pyramids. These structures, known far and wide in the ancient world, even in Babylon, were a great wonder and showcased the might of this river civilization.

However, these pyramids, despite their magnificence, were not the reason Sumshir ventured forth from Babylon and came to these far lands. For ze was a trader and knew the cities around the pyramids produced the best faiences that could be bought with coin. These works of glazed earthenware often made into jewelry were becoming more and more popular in many lands Sumshir traveled from. And so, ze wished to find a trading partner in these cities who could be trusted to send these ceramic faiences by caravan.

Sumshir had walked a good distance along the river when ze saw a youthful person in a small boat coming to shore. Sumshir knew their manners and helped the youth pull the boat ashore by meeting it in the shallow water and pulling it onto the bank just enough so it would not drift away. When almost the entire length of the boat was on dry sand, Sumshir saw a bountiful pile of fish on the floor of the boat. These fish were much bigger than the ones their caravan had been buying on this long journey of many moons.

“Thank you, my friend,” the young fisherfolk said, their face beaming with a grin reaching their ears.

“Helping others is one of life’s little joys,” said Sumshir, panting a bit from pulling the boat. “I say, this is an abundant harvest. How did thou find such plentiful fish in this river? My caravan could only catch fish half this size since we found the river eight days ago.”

“Ah, my friend, that is a secret one can only learn by living on the riverbanks from an early age. And even if I tell you, it may take me a lifetime to explain it,” the fisherfolk winked and made a soft smile.

“Well said,” Sumshir chuckled. “Then, I shall no longer ask, but I do wonder, what does such an efficient fisherfolk like thee do to make coin? With thou being able to pull in such a fine catch, it makes a person wonder if thou does also catch coins. With the sun rising, are thou about to go to work?”

“My catching of fish is done for the day. Now, I am returning home to my family.”

“Ah, thou must be a person wise in the handling of coin if thou can earn while not laboring under another’s employ,” Sumshir said with high praise.

“Wrong again, my new friend,” the fisher fellow said with laughter. “I still need a little coin. I catch fish in the morning, sell it, come home and play with my children, and sing songs with my good spouse while ze tends to our herb garden. I have a full life, but not a busy life. I have little need for more coin than the few I use."

"So, thou do not dedicate a portion of each day to the practice of making coin?"

The fisherfolk could heed the slight hint of exasperation in Sumshir's voice. "No, I do not."

"Then, my friend, what wouldst thou do if thy good spouse was to fall ill? Or, gods forsake me, if one of thy children gets a cut on their foot and the rot sets in? Even if thou were to hire a healer, they seldom work without an exchange of coin."

The smile on the young fisherfolk left their face, and the lids of their eyes dropped. "You may be right about the last part. But my spouse has good health, and we pray to the gods each night for the health of my kids."

Sumshir could sense a brewing discomfort from the young fisher's expression and deep voice. Still the trader could not help but express concern. "My companions say each year, the monsoon season causes the Nile to flood and overflow its banks. I heard stories of the horrors of such floods this supposed river of life inflicts on the inhabitants near the river. Do they not pray for the gods to protect them as well?"

The fisherfolk's eyebrows furrowed and ze flashed zir eyes at Sumshir. "My friend, you are but a foreigner here. You know little about the lives of the folk who live in these blessed lands. What you speak of is not something I think about," the youth paused, then eyed a large, long stake lying on the sand. "I regret I cannot keep you company for long. I must go now."

The fisherfolk picked up the stake and drove it into the ground. Ze grabbed a rope tied to the front of the boat, took the other end, and tied that end around the stake to keep the boat from drifting away, even though it was nearly out of the water. Ze then wiped the sweat on their forehead with the back of their hand, which ze then wiped on their wet and tattered shendyt tied around the waist. Afterward and without a word, the young fisherfolk walked away with the catch.

As Sumshir was left alone again by the shore, their heart felt heavy. Ze felt the fisherfolk had a much promising future had the youth taken their advice. If misfortune should befall this fellow and their family, they would have little recourse for survival without enough coin to spare.

Then again, Sumshir realized ze might have been too imposing and caused the youth to clam up and stop their ears and mind from listening to others. Sumshir thought the fisherfolk raised a good point; Sumshir was a foreigner, and ze might have acted like an invading army to the fisherfolk's eyes; first seeking diplomacy, then demanding tribute and, eventually, conquering their lands.

Not wanting to overthink, Sumshir shook their head and continued walking along the riverbank. Up ahead, ze saw more fisherfolk going about their day, some counting their morning catch and some mending their nets. Sumshir decided to approach and talk to them.

From their conversations, Sumshir learned that despite the Nile's annual monsoon floods that threatened these people's lives and livelihoods, such occurrences also brought many benefits. These floods often carry silt from the upriver. Farmers near the banks would use this fertile silt to help with agriculture.

Hearing this information, Sumshir thanked the fisherfolk and went back to the caravan. Later that day, Sumshir learned some traders from Egypt wanted to travel with them. And so, the caravan had to remain for a couple more days to wait for these lagging traders to catch up.

The next morning, Sumshir walked along the riverbank again when ze spotted the same young fisherfolk on the river. The fisherfolk waved at them, and with a slow, rhythmic paddle, the fisherfolk beached the small boat. Sumshir once again, following local customs, helped pull the boat out of the water.

"My friend," the fisherfolk greeted, their voice calmer this time than yesterday, "I pray our previous conversation had gone without any ill will, and if it did, my sincere apologies. When yesterday I went home and spoke to my good spouse, I did not know this about the love of my life, but they had the same concerns as you. We talked until the sun began to set. I must admit, after speaking with my spouse, I have now begun a thoughtful reflection on the words you spoke to me.

"But, my new friend, I cannot work like the others do. I cannot go to a shack and hammer stone after stone to make the coin. But we have a saying in this village: advice is worth what you pay for it. So, this morning, I caught four big fish just for you. Now, pray tell, what advice do you have for a simple person like me for the price of four of the finest fish from this river?"

Sumshir smiled and stared off into the water once more. "Well, let me ponder for a moment," ze said with a brief pause. "See, there are two directions thou can take, and at this moment without knowing more of thy situation, I find it hard to pick one and say it is correct. So, I will explain both and thou can find the path best for thee."

Leaning on one side of the wooden boat, Sumshir looked at the distance and saw another boat with a furrowed sail and a rowing crew. "Getting into a business creates an opportunity for thee to have coins ready to invest in wise investments. A good rule of thumb is for every ten coins thou earn, thou shall save one to invest into thy future.

"But, my young friend, in thy simple lifestyle without much want, thou are at a unique advantage. Since thou earn little coin today, if thou shall start putting thy mind and body towards the pursuit of making coin, thou will have much excess even if thou does save only one of ten coins. Thus, I suggest this: when thou start working, save six out of ten coins for thee to make wise investments in. Then, take and use two of the remaining coins to live thy life and prosper. How does that sound so far?"

After a moment, the fisherfolk replied, "My knowledge of numbers does not deceive me. What shall I do with the extra two coins?"

Sumshir smiled, "Very observant. These remaining coins will take us to the second path, which involves training other people in thy trade and teaching them thy fishing techniques. Since they work under thy employment, thou can take a portion of their catch each day, for it is important to separate thy income from the hours thou gives into it.

"Suppose the wood on thy boat splinters and thou does get a cut on thy hand. Thou may become gravely injured or ill. When these things happen, thou may no longer fish or find it difficult to do so. Then, thou will no longer have a stream of coin to fill thy purse, and thy good spouse may go hungry until thou have healed.

"Now, suppose thou has a crew of two fishing in the river each day. This will allow thee to continue receiving coin without using thy body to do the work."

"That is a good point you raise, my friend," the young fellow said. "But that still does not answer what happens with the two spare coins."

"Do thou not see it? These coins are thy payment to thy crew! Each time thou does fish with them and sell thy catch, thou pays these coins to them as compensation for working for thee." Sumshir paused before continuing, "This task is not as easy as it may seem, my friend. Many people may own a business, but they still need to work for the business to create money. Thou must set up thy venture so that even when thou do need to leave the river for a week, the business still runs without thee. Whereas if thou own a business but still has to work in the business each day to make coin, thou simply own their own job. Thou must separate themselves from the actual work of the business, so that it can make coin without thee."

The fisherfolk took a moment to digest the things Sumshir said, but at the very least, the youth was no longer apprehensive about the trader's idea. "In other words," the fisherfolk said, "I must make my business earn coin for me even if I, as the owner, am no longer working?"

With a beaming face resembling that of a proud parent smiling for their child's accomplishment, Sumshir said, "Precisely, my young friend."

Soon after their conversation, Sumshir bade farewell to the fisherfolk and returned to the caravan. The next day, the Egyptian traders caught up, and the caravan broke camp and finally left. With the four large fish the youth paid, Sumshir managed to have enough to eat and share with a few other travelers during the journey back to Babylon.

Several months later, Sumshir returned to Egypt bringing another batch of goods. The caravan ze rode with stopped by the same stretch of the Nile where Sumshir encountered the same fisherfolk in the previous journey. Sumshir saw the youth again who, this time around, was fishing with two people aboard the boat.

Sumshir and the fisher fellow conversed for a brief while, with the youth explaining how ze managed to hire two fishers last month.

"Since the past two moons," the young fisherfolk said with a grin, "our catch has been twice more than what I normally get in the past, when I used to fish alone. Of course, I pay my companions two-tenths of what I earn from selling the fish, as you suggested. Now I am saving the excess of what my family spends and learning more about investing money as I go."

Pleased, Sumshir imparted a few more lessons to the youth before leaving with the caravan again. Then, after several more months, Sumshir returned. This time, the trader was wide-eyed upon seeing the young fisherfolk once more.

The fisherfolk, this time garbed in a clean, white, pleated shendyt that contrasted the tattered and torn ones ze used to wear back when they first met greeted Sumshir. From the youth's appearance, Sumshir deduced this fellow now had enough money to buy new clothes.

The trader also noticed something else about the youth. "Thou seem to be working less," Sumshir said. "Thy garments are clean, and despite coming from a fresh catch, thou are not wet from the water or sweat."

"It is as you say," the fisherfolk said. Ze pointed toward the part of the riverbank where ze used to pull their small boat back to shore. The boat was no longer there, but in its place were two mid-sized boats. "See, I sold my old boat, and with the spare money I saved, I hired more people and bought two new boats. With more hands, I earn more and do more without spending as much time fishing as before."

Again, Sumshir commended the young fisherfolk for these

achievements. But before Sumshir left to continue with their business, the youth told him of the current situation among the other folk near the riverbank.

"Some of these people want to fish but do not have the coin to buy a boat," the fellow said. "We plan on buying a boat and letting some of them use it to fish until they pay for it."

Hearing the young fisherfolk explain this made Sumshir glad ze had imparted their wisdom on this enterprising individual. Determined to teach the youth even further, Sumshir invited them to travel south to visit more people along the Nile who might want boats as well.

As Sumshir expected, they encountered more people wanting to fish but lacking the coin needed to purchase the boats. Thus, Sumshir assisted the young fisherfolk's venture to buy more boats. They visited several boatbuilders and arranged contracts to supply or build the vessels.

Sumshir left once again and would not come back until about six months later.

When ze returned to Egypt and visited the young fisher following that period, Sumshir had to rub and squint their eyes, for ze was unsure whether what ze saw was real or a mirage.

"By the gods!" Sumshir exclaimed, watching six mid-sized boats anchored out in the water near the shore. "Thou have four more?"

The young fisherfolk chuckled and crossed their arms. "With two more arriving in a couple of months."

Sumshir could not help but laugh. "Are thou starting a naval fleet, my friend? The whole of Egypt might tremble!"

"I am sure you simply joke, but all these would have not been fulfilled had I not taken your wise words. Now, not only am I employing several hands to catch fish and earn me money, but I am also helping my neighbors fish for themselves as well. Furthermore, I am saving enough for my future. Should any calamity or ill circumstance happen, I believe my family and I will manage to see things through."

For the next few months, Sumshir continued traveling with the caravan to trade goods between Babylon and Egypt. After a few years, Sumshir found the fisher fellow had become rather wealthy, thanks to the concept of investments. The fisher's fleet grew and ze no longer worked the job. Instead, ze spent their days playing with their kids in safety and prosperity.

Sumshir spent many nights along the banks of the Nile reflecting the great difference between owning one's job and owning their business.

This is the end of this story. If thou wish to live life with great liberality, then this is the beginning of yours.

A THANK YOU LETTER TO GEORGE S. CLASON

Thank you for writing The Richest Person in Babylon. I listened to this audiobook, and it made my heart race with excitement. Then, a month later, I got laid off for the first time in my life, within months of liquidating all of my savings to pay off my student loans, nonetheless. What followed was four years of living below the poverty line until I became a person of means again (with a chunk of credit card debt to get through). I did what the book said, and I saved a percentage of my income, and that savings allowed me to afford to go out and get proper employment, trim my financial burdens, retain my income, and devise ways to obtain future income, most of all.

I would say the greatest thing this book gave me is it showed me what financial education is, unleashing the flood gates of self-education. This opened up a new paradigm of life in which I could learn how to gain wealth. While I was laid off periodically in the coming years, several thoughts kept coming to me.

Paraphrasing:

“A brick maker gives poor knowledge about diamonds but gives great knowledge regarding bricks!”

“… a person wants to be a merchant and doesn’t know where to buy cheap and sell high? Ze won’t say, ‘I will go to Egypt and buy from the merchants of the Nile, from the sunrise side and near the sea. Then haul in caravan to Damascus to sell to the house people of the silver smiths, apothecaries, and nobility.’ Pfft, I pity fool…”

"You need to secure a future income. It is what is most important."

I wish to live life with great liberality.

Published 2025 by Evoking Quality Publishing

Previously published as The Richest Man in Babylon

Original publication date: 1926
Republication date: 2025

Printed in: United States of America

Made in the USA
Monee, IL
06 November 2026

68012407R00135